Eilish E Culinary Symphony of 98 Inspired Recipes

Cucumber Oregano Olive Oil

Contents

INTRODUCTION

"Eilish Eats: A Culinary Symphony of 98 Inspired Recipes" invites you into the vibrant, eclectic world of Billie Eilish through the lens of culinary artistry. This cookbook is a celebration of creativity, individuality, and the flavors that resonate with the essence of this musical sensation.

With 98 meticulously crafted recipes, each dish is a melodic fusion of taste, style, and innovation inspired by Billie Eilish's music, personality, and journey. From comforting classics to avant-garde creations, this cookbook reflects the diverse and unconventional nature of Billie's artistry.

The culinary journey begins by delving into the rich tapestry of Billie's life and music, drawing inspiration from her evocative lyrics, bold fashion choices, and unapologetic attitude. Each recipe is an ode to her spirit—be it a dish that echoes the nostalgia of her childhood or a bold, unexpected flavor combination that mirrors her fearless approach to creativity.

Embracing the ethos of individuality, "Eilish Eats" encourages culinary exploration. Whether you're a novice or an experienced chef, these recipes cater to all skill levels, inviting you to experiment, improvise, and infuse your own personal flair into each dish.

The cookbook is a symphony of flavors, meticulously curated into chapters that reflect different aspects of Billie's life and artistry. Indulge in "Ocean Eyes Eats" for dishes that evoke a sense of serenity and depth. "Bad Guy Bites" explores edgy and unconventional flavors that challenge the palate. "Green Hair Grazes" celebrates plant-based recipes that echo Billie's commitment to sustainability and wellness.

Expect an array of recipes that span from delectable breakfast creations like "Bellyache Brunch Pancakes" to savory delights such as "Bury a Friend Bolognese" and "Lovely Lemon Risotto." Satisfy your sweet tooth with desserts like "Billie's Bite-Sized Baked Goods" and "When the Party's Over Popsicles."

Beyond the recipes, "Eilish Eats" is a visual feast, adorned with stunning photography capturing the essence of each dish and the energy of Billie's persona. The anecdotes woven throughout the book offer glimpses into the inspirations behind the recipes, creating a deeper connection between the food and Billie's world.

This cookbook isn't just about food; it's an exploration of artistry, individualism, and the unapologetic celebration of self. It invites you to embrace the unexpected, to savor the unconventional, and to revel in the magic of both food and music.

"Eilish Eats: A Culinary Symphony of 98 Inspired Recipes" is more than a collection of dishes—it's a culinary journey that mirrors the soulful melodies and vibrant hues of Billie Eilish's remarkable presence in the world. It's an invitation to step into her world through the art of cooking, to embrace creativity, and to savor every bite of this symphony of flavors.

1. Bad Guy Black Bean Soup

Dive into the dark and flavorful world of Billie Eilish with our "Bad Guy Black Bean Soup." Inspired by the haunting beats and soulful lyrics of Billie's music, this soup is a celebration of bold flavors and unique textures. Get ready to embark on a culinary journey that mirrors the eclectic nature of Billie's music, with every spoonful taking you deeper into the mysterious depths of taste.

Serving: 4 servings
Preparation Time: 15 minutes
Ready Time: 45 minutes

Ingredients:
- 2 cans (15 oz each) black beans, drained and rinsed
- 1 tablespoon olive oil
- 1 onion, finely chopped
- 3 cloves garlic, minced
- 1 red bell pepper, diced
- 1 teaspoon ground cumin
- 1 teaspoon smoked paprika
- 1/2 teaspoon chili powder
- 4 cups vegetable broth
- 1 can (14 oz) diced tomatoes
- Salt and pepper to taste
- 1 cup corn kernels (fresh or frozen)
- 1 lime, juiced
- Fresh cilantro, chopped, for garnish
- Avocado slices, for garnish
- Sour cream, for garnish (optional)

Instructions:
1. In a large pot, heat the olive oil over medium heat. Add the chopped onion and cook until translucent, about 3-5 minutes.
2. Add the minced garlic and diced red bell pepper to the pot. Sauté for an additional 2-3 minutes until the pepper begins to soften.
3. Sprinkle in the ground cumin, smoked paprika, and chili powder. Stir to coat the vegetables in the spices.

4. Pour in the vegetable broth, black beans, and diced tomatoes with their juices. Season with salt and pepper to taste. Bring the soup to a simmer and let it cook for 20-25 minutes.

5. Add the corn kernels to the soup and continue to simmer for an additional 10-15 minutes, allowing the flavors to meld together.

6. Just before serving, stir in the lime juice for a burst of freshness.

7. Ladle the "Bad Guy Black Bean Soup" into bowls and garnish with chopped cilantro, avocado slices, and a dollop of sour cream if desired.

Nutrition Information:
(Per serving)
- Calories: 320
- Total Fat: 6g
- Saturated Fat: 1g
- Trans Fat: 0g
- Cholesterol: 0mg
- Sodium: 850mg
- Total Carbohydrates: 58g
- Dietary Fiber: 15g
- Sugars: 7g
- Protein: 15g

Immerse yourself in the rich flavors of this "Bad Guy Black Bean Soup," a culinary homage to the enigmatic and soul-stirring artistry of Billie Eilish. Each spoonful is a symphony of tastes, making it the perfect dish for those who appreciate a bit of darkness in their culinary repertoire.

2. Ocean Eyes Octopus Sushi

Inspired by the hauntingly beautiful song "Ocean Eyes" by Billie Eilish, this Ocean Eyes Octopus Sushi is a culinary tribute to the mesmerizing depths of the ocean. With a creative twist on traditional sushi, this dish combines the flavors of the sea with a touch of elegance, making it a perfect choice for those who appreciate both artistry and gastronomy.

Serving: 4 rolls
Preparation Time: 30 minutes
Ready Time: 1 hour

Ingredients:
- 2 cups sushi rice, cooked and seasoned
- 4 sheets nori (seaweed)
- 1 octopus, cooked and thinly sliced
- 1 cucumber, julienned
- 1 avocado, sliced
- Soy sauce for dipping
- Pickled ginger for serving
- Wasabi for serving
- Sesame seeds for garnish
- Nori strips for decoration

Instructions:
1. Prepare the Rice:
- Cook the sushi rice according to package instructions.
- Once cooked, let it cool to room temperature.
- Season the rice with rice vinegar, sugar, and salt, mixing gently.
2. Assemble the Sushi Rolls:
- Place a bamboo sushi rolling mat on a clean surface.
- Lay a sheet of nori on the mat, shiny side down.
- Wet your hands to prevent sticking and spread a thin layer of rice over the nori, leaving a small border at the top.
- Arrange slices of octopus, cucumber, and avocado along the bottom edge of the rice.
3. Rolling the Sushi:
- Lift the bottom edge of the bamboo mat with your thumbs while keeping the fillings in place with your fingers.
- Roll the mat away from you, forming a tight cylinder.
- Seal the edge of the nori with a small amount of water.
4. Slice and Garnish:
- Using a sharp, wet knife, slice the roll into bite-sized pieces.
- Arrange the sushi on a plate and garnish with sesame seeds and nori strips for an artistic touch.
5. Serve:
- Serve the Ocean Eyes Octopus Sushi with soy sauce, pickled ginger, and wasabi on the side.

Nutrition Information:
(Per Serving)
- Calories: 320

- Protein: 15g
- Carbohydrates: 60g
- Fat: 5g
- Fiber: 5g
- Sugar: 2g

Indulge in the symphony of flavors and textures that make up this Ocean Eyes Octopus Sushi, a dish that pays homage to Billie Eilish's ethereal musical world. Enjoy the harmony of the ocean on your plate!

3. When The Party's Over Blueberry Smoothie

Indulge your taste buds in the ethereal and melancholic vibes of Billie Eilish with the "When The Party's Over Blueberry Smoothie." This vibrant concoction captures the essence of Billie's soulful melodies and provides a refreshing burst of flavor that's perfect for any occasion. Packed with antioxidants and a symphony of delightful ingredients, this smoothie is a melody of goodness that will leave you craving more.

Serving: 2 servings
Preparation Time: 10 minutes
Ready Time: 10 minutes

Ingredients:
- 1 cup frozen blueberries
- 1 ripe banana
- 1/2 cup vanilla yogurt
- 1/2 cup almond milk (or any milk of your choice)
- 1 tablespoon honey (adjust to taste)
- 1/2 teaspoon chia seeds
- A handful of ice cubes
- Edible flowers for garnish (optional)

Instructions:
1. Blend the Melody:
- In a blender, combine the frozen blueberries, ripe banana, vanilla yogurt, almond milk, honey, and chia seeds.
2. Smooth Symphony:

- Blend the ingredients until smooth and creamy. If the consistency is too thick, you can add more almond milk to reach your desired thickness.
3. Chill Vibes:
- Add the ice cubes and blend again until the ice is fully incorporated, creating a cool and refreshing texture.
4. Taste the Harmony:
- Taste the smoothie and adjust the sweetness by adding more honey if needed. Blend briefly to combine.
5. Pour and Garnish:
- Pour the smoothie into glasses and garnish with edible flowers if desired, adding a touch of visual flair to your drink.
6. Serve with Eilish Vibes:
- Serve immediately, embracing the cool and captivating vibes of Billie Eilish as you enjoy every sip of this enchanting blueberry smoothie.

Nutrition Information (per serving):
- Calories: 180
- Protein: 3g
- Fat: 2g
- Carbohydrates: 40g
- Fiber: 5g
- Sugar: 26g
- Vitamin C: 16mg
- Calcium: 150mg
- Iron: 1mg
Note: Nutrition information is approximate and may vary based on specific ingredients and brands used.

4. Bellyache Berry Salad

Indulge your taste buds in the whimsical world of Billie Eilish with our "Bellyache Berry Salad." This vibrant and refreshing salad pays homage to Billie's hit song "Bellyache," combining a medley of berries that will make your palate sing. Bursting with color and flavor, this salad is not only a feast for the senses but also a nod to Billie's eclectic and bold style. Get ready to experience the symphony of tastes in every bite!

Serving: 4 servings

Preparation Time: 15 minutes
Ready Time: 20 minutes

Ingredients:
- 2 cups fresh strawberries, hulled and halved
- 1 cup fresh blueberries
- 1 cup fresh raspberries
- 1 cup fresh blackberries
- 1/4 cup chopped fresh mint leaves
- 1/2 cup crumbled feta cheese
- 1/4 cup chopped walnuts, toasted
Dressing:
- 2 tablespoons honey
- 2 tablespoons balsamic vinegar
- 1 tablespoon extra-virgin olive oil
- 1 teaspoon Dijon mustard
- Salt and pepper to taste

Instructions:
1. Prepare the Berries: In a large bowl, combine the strawberries, blueberries, raspberries, and blackberries.
2. Add the Freshness: Gently fold in the chopped mint leaves to add a burst of freshness to the mix.
3. Create the Dressing: In a small bowl, whisk together honey, balsamic vinegar, olive oil, Dijon mustard, salt, and pepper until well combined.
4. Toss and Dress: Drizzle the dressing over the berries and toss gently to coat them evenly.
5. Top with Goodies: Sprinkle the crumbled feta cheese and toasted walnuts over the salad for a delightful texture and nutty undertones.
6. Chill (Optional): Refrigerate for 5 minutes if you prefer a slightly chilled salad.
7. Serve: Divide the Bellyache Berry Salad among four plates and serve immediately.

Nutrition Information (per serving):
- Calories: 180
- Total Fat: 10g
- Saturated Fat: 3g
- Trans Fat: 0g
- Cholesterol: 15mg

- Sodium: 120mg
- Total Carbohydrates: 21g
- Dietary Fiber: 6g
- Sugars: 13g
- Protein: 4g

Enjoy the Bellyache Berry Salad, a harmonious blend of flavors that captures the essence of Billie Eilish's creativity and style. This dish is not only a treat for your taste buds but also a visual masterpiece that reflects the vibrancy of Billie's music.

5. Bury A Friend Burrito Bowl

Step into the dark and tantalizing world of Billie Eilish with the "Bury A Friend Burrito Bowl." This dish pays homage to the hauntingly beautiful vibes of Billie's music, blending bold flavors and textures to create a culinary experience that's as unique as her sound. Get ready to embark on a flavorful journey inspired by the one and only Billie Eilish.

Serving: 4
Preparation time: 20 minutes
Ready time: 30 minutes

Ingredients:
- 1 cup quinoa, cooked
- 1 can black beans, drained and rinsed
- 1 cup corn kernels, fresh or frozen
- 1 cup cherry tomatoes, halved
- 1 avocado, sliced
- 1 cup purple cabbage, thinly shredded
- 1 cup red onion, finely diced
- 1 cup fresh cilantro, chopped
- 1 lime, cut into wedges
For the Chipotle Lime Dressing:
- 1/4 cup olive oil
- 2 tablespoons lime juice
- 1 tablespoon honey
- 1 teaspoon chipotle chili powder
- 1 teaspoon cumin

- Salt and pepper to taste

Instructions:
1. Prepare Quinoa: Cook quinoa according to package instructions. Once cooked, fluff it with a fork and set aside.
2. Make Chipotle Lime Dressing: In a small bowl, whisk together olive oil, lime juice, honey, chipotle chili powder, cumin, salt, and pepper. Set aside.
3. Assemble Burrito Bowl: In individual serving bowls, layer the cooked quinoa, black beans, corn, cherry tomatoes, avocado slices, shredded purple cabbage, and diced red onion.
4. Drizzle with Dressing: Pour the chipotle lime dressing over the assembled burrito bowls.
5. Garnish: Sprinkle chopped cilantro on top and add a lime wedge to each bowl.
6. Serve: Serve the "Bury A Friend Burrito Bowl" immediately, allowing each person to mix the ingredients and dressing to their liking.

Nutrition Information:
(Per Serving)
- Calories: 450
- Protein: 12g
- Carbohydrates: 60g
- Fiber: 14g
- Sugar: 8g
- Fat: 20g
- Saturated Fat: 3g
- Cholesterol: 0mg
- Sodium: 320mg
- Vitamin D: 0mcg
- Calcium: 80mg
- Iron: 4mg
- Potassium: 1020mg

Let the "Bury A Friend Burrito Bowl" transport you to a world of bold flavors and vibrant colors, inspired by the incredible Billie Eilish. Enjoy the fusion of textures and tastes as you savor this musical masterpiece on a plate!

6. Copycat Avocado Toast

Channeling the eclectic and vibrant spirit of the sensational Billie Eilish, we bring you a delightful rendition of the iconic Avocado Toast. This Copycat Avocado Toast captures the essence of Billie's bold style and unique flair. With creamy avocado, zesty seasoning, and a touch of inspiration, this dish is a perfect embodiment of Billie's creativity on your plate. Get ready to indulge in a symphony of flavors that mirror the multifaceted artistry of this musical sensation.

Serving: Serves 2
Preparation Time: 15 minutes
Ready Time: 15 minutes

Ingredients:
- 2 ripe avocados
- 4 slices of your favorite bread (sourdough, whole grain, or gluten-free, as per preference)
- 1 lemon, juiced
- 1 teaspoon red pepper flakes (adjust to taste)
- Salt and pepper to taste
- 2 tablespoons extra virgin olive oil
- Optional toppings: cherry tomatoes, radishes, microgreens, or a poached egg

Instructions:
1. Avocado Mash:
- Cut the avocados in half, remove the pits, and scoop the flesh into a bowl.
- Mash the avocados with a fork until you achieve your desired consistency.
- Add the freshly squeezed lemon juice, red pepper flakes, salt, and pepper. Mix well.
2. Toast the Bread:
- Toast the bread slices to your liking. You can use a toaster, toaster oven, or a conventional oven.
3. Assemble:
- Spread a generous layer of the avocado mixture onto each toasted slice of bread.
4. Season and Garnish:

- Drizzle extra virgin olive oil over the avocado spread.
- Sprinkle additional red pepper flakes, if desired, for an extra kick.
- Add your favorite toppings, such as cherry tomatoes, radishes, microgreens, or a poached egg.
5. Serve:
- Arrange the prepared avocado toasts on a plate and serve immediately.

Nutrition Information:
(Per Serving)
- Calories: 350
- Total Fat: 22g
- Saturated Fat: 3g
- Trans Fat: 0g
- Cholesterol: 0mg
- Sodium: 300mg
- Total Carbohydrates: 35g
- Dietary Fiber: 12g
- Sugars: 3g
- Protein: 7g
Note: Nutrition information may vary based on the type of bread and optional toppings used.
Elevate your breakfast or brunch experience with this Copycat Avocado Toast inspired by the musical genius, Billie Eilish. It's a harmonious blend of flavors that will leave you craving more, just like the unforgettable tunes from this iconic artist.

7. All The Good Girls Go To Hell Guacamole

Indulge your taste buds in a rebellious symphony of flavors with "All The Good Girls Go To Hell Guacamole," a culinary creation inspired by the iconic Billie Eilish. This guacamole is a tribute to the artist's bold and unapologetic style, combining creamy avocados with a medley of vibrant ingredients that dance on your palate. Dive into this unique blend of textures and tastes, and let your taste buds revel in the rebellious spirit of Billie Eilish.

Serving: Perfect for sharing at gatherings or as a solo snack while you immerse yourself in Billie's music. This recipe yields approximately 2 cups of guacamole.
Preparation Time: 15 minutes
Ready Time: 15 minutes

Ingredients:
- 3 ripe avocados
- 1 small red onion, finely diced
- 1-2 jalapeños, seeded and minced
- 2 cloves garlic, minced
- 1 large tomato, diced
- 1/4 cup fresh cilantro, chopped
- Juice of 2 limes
- Salt and pepper to taste
- Tortilla chips for serving

Instructions:
1. Prepare the Avocados: Cut the avocados in half, remove the pits, and scoop the flesh into a bowl.
2. Mash the Avocados: Using a fork or potato masher, mash the avocados to your desired consistency—some like it chunky, while others prefer it smoother.
3. Add Aromatic Vegetables: Stir in the diced red onion, minced jalapeños, and garlic. These ingredients add a kick to your guacamole.
4. Incorporate Tomato and Cilantro: Gently fold in the diced tomato and chopped cilantro, providing freshness and color to the mix.
5. Lime Infusion: Squeeze the juice of two limes into the bowl, ensuring a zesty and citrusy undertone to your guacamole.
6. Season to Perfection: Sprinkle salt and pepper over the guacamole, adjusting the seasoning according to your taste preferences. Mix well.
7. Serve: Transfer the guacamole to a serving dish and surround it with your favorite tortilla chips.
8. Enjoy: Dive into the flavorful rebellion of "All The Good Girls Go To Hell Guacamole" and savor the unique blend inspired by Billie Eilish.

Nutrition Information:
(Per 1/4 cup serving)
- Calories: 120
- Total Fat: 10g

- Saturated Fat: 1.5g
- Cholesterol: 0mg
- Sodium: 150mg
- Total Carbohydrates: 8g
- Dietary Fiber: 4g
- Sugars: 1g
- Protein: 2g

Note: Nutrition information is approximate and may vary based on specific ingredients used.

8. My Strange Addiction Miso Soup

Indulge your taste buds in a symphony of flavors with "My Strange Addiction Miso Soup," inspired by the eclectic palette of Billie Eilish. This unique twist on traditional miso soup combines unexpected ingredients to create a culinary masterpiece that mirrors Billie's avant-garde approach to music.

Serving: 4 bowls
Preparation time: 15 minutes
Ready time: 30 minutes

Ingredients:
- 4 cups dashi stock (homemade or store-bought)
- 1/3 cup miso paste (white or red)
- 1 cup firm tofu, cubed
- 1 cup shiitake mushrooms, sliced
- 1 cup wakame seaweed, soaked and chopped
- 1 tablespoon soy sauce
- 1 teaspoon sesame oil
- 2 green onions, finely chopped
- 1 teaspoon grated fresh ginger
- 1 clove garlic, minced
- 1 tablespoon rice vinegar
- 1 teaspoon chili oil (optional, for an extra kick)
- Cooked white rice (optional, for serving)

Instructions:

1. Prepare the Dashi Stock:
- If using homemade dashi, follow your preferred recipe. Alternatively, heat store-bought dashi in a pot over medium heat.
2. Dissolve Miso Paste:
- In a small bowl, dissolve the miso paste in a ladleful of the hot dashi. Whisk until smooth.
3. Add Tofu and Mushrooms:
- Add the cubed tofu and sliced shiitake mushrooms to the simmering dashi. Cook until the mushrooms are tender, about 5 minutes.
4. Incorporate Remaining Ingredients:
- Stir in the wakame seaweed, soy sauce, sesame oil, green onions, grated ginger, minced garlic, rice vinegar, and chili oil if desired. Let it simmer for an additional 5-7 minutes.
5. Blend in Miso Paste:
- Lower the heat and gradually whisk in the dissolved miso paste. Avoid boiling the soup after adding the miso to preserve its delicate flavor.
6. Adjust Seasoning:
- Taste the soup and adjust the seasoning if necessary, adding more soy sauce or miso paste according to your preference.
7. Serve:
- Ladle the My Strange Addiction Miso Soup into bowls. If desired, serve over a bed of cooked white rice.

Nutrition Information:
Per Serving (1 bowl):
- Calories: 120
- Total Fat: 6g
- Saturated Fat: 1g
- Trans Fat: 0g
- Cholesterol: 0mg
- Sodium: 800mg
- Total Carbohydrates: 12g
- Dietary Fiber: 2g
- Sugars: 2g
- Protein: 8g

Indulge in the harmony of flavors and textures in this My Strange Addiction Miso Soup, a delightful homage to the innovative spirit of Billie Eilish.

9. Ilomilo Ice Cream Sandwiches

Get ready to indulge in the whimsical world of Billie Eilish with these delightful Ilomilo Ice Cream Sandwiches. Named after the enchanting track, these treats are a perfect blend of sweet and nostalgic, just like Billie's music. With a crunchy exterior and a creamy interior, these ice cream sandwiches are a sensory journey, echoing the eclectic vibes of Billie Eilish's artistry.

Serving: Makes approximately 12 Ilomilo Ice Cream Sandwiches
Preparation Time: 15 minutes
Ready Time: 4 hours (includes freezing time)

Ingredients:
- 2 cups all-purpose flour
- 1 teaspoon baking soda
- 1/2 teaspoon salt
- 3/4 cup unsalted butter, softened
- 1 cup brown sugar, packed
- 1/2 cup granulated sugar
- 2 large eggs
- 2 teaspoons vanilla extract
- 2 cups chocolate chips
- 1.5 quarts of your favorite ice cream (vanilla, chocolate, or a flavor inspired by Billie Eilish's favorites)

Instructions:
1. Preheat the Oven:
Preheat your oven to 350°F (175°C). Line a baking sheet with parchment paper.
2. Combine Dry Ingredients:
In a medium bowl, whisk together the flour, baking soda, and salt. Set aside.
3. Cream the Butter and Sugars:
In a large mixing bowl, cream together the softened butter, brown sugar, and granulated sugar until light and fluffy.
4. Add Eggs and Vanilla:
Beat in the eggs, one at a time, ensuring each is fully incorporated before adding the next. Add the vanilla extract and mix well.
5. Incorporate Dry Ingredients:

Gradually add the dry ingredients to the wet ingredients, mixing until just combined. Fold in the chocolate chips.

6. Form Cookie Dough Balls:

Scoop tablespoon-sized portions of cookie dough and place them on the prepared baking sheet, leaving space between each.

7. Bake:

Bake in the preheated oven for 10-12 minutes or until the edges are golden brown. Allow the cookies to cool on the baking sheet for a few minutes before transferring them to a wire rack to cool completely.

8. Assemble Ice Cream Sandwiches:

Once the cookies are completely cooled, scoop a generous amount of ice cream onto the flat side of one cookie. Top it with another cookie, creating a sandwich. Repeat until all cookies are used.

9. Freeze:

Place the assembled ice cream sandwiches in the freezer for at least 3-4 hours or until the ice cream is firm.

10. Serve:

Remove from the freezer, let them sit for a minute or two to soften slightly, and enjoy these Ilomilo Ice Cream Sandwiches inspired by the musical magic of Billie Eilish!

Nutrition Information:

Note: Nutritional values are approximate and may vary based on specific ingredients and ice cream flavors used.

- Calories per serving: ~320 kcal
- Total Fat: ~18g
- Saturated Fat: ~11g
- Cholesterol: ~70mg
- Sodium: ~150mg
- Total Carbohydrates: ~38g
- Dietary Fiber: ~1g
- Sugars: ~26g
- Protein: ~3g

Enjoy this sweet treat that's as unique and captivating as Billie Eilish's music!

10. Everything I Wanted Eggplant Parmesan

Indulge in the melodious symphony of flavors with "Everything I Wanted Eggplant Parmesan," a dish inspired by the eclectic and daring spirit of Billie Eilish. This culinary creation is a fusion of rich textures and bold tastes, capturing the essence of Billie's innovative style. Get ready to embark on a culinary journey that mirrors the depth and complexity of her music.

Serving: Serves 4
Preparation Time: 20 minutes
Ready Time: 1 hour

Ingredients:
- 2 large eggplants, sliced into 1/2-inch rounds
- 2 cups breadcrumbs
- 1 cup grated Parmesan cheese
- 4 cups marinara sauce
- 2 cups shredded mozzarella cheese
- 1 cup fresh basil leaves, torn
- 1 teaspoon dried oregano
- 1 teaspoon garlic powder
- Salt and pepper to taste
- Olive oil for baking

Instructions:
1. Preheat the Oven:
Preheat your oven to 375°F (190°C).
2. Prepare the Eggplant:
a. Sprinkle eggplant slices with salt and let them sit for 15 minutes to draw out excess moisture.
b. Pat the eggplant slices dry with paper towels.
3. Breading the Eggplant:
a. In a shallow dish, combine breadcrumbs, grated Parmesan, dried oregano, and garlic powder.
b. Dredge each eggplant slice in the breadcrumb mixture, ensuring they are evenly coated.
4. Bake the Eggplant:
a. Place the breaded eggplant slices on a baking sheet.
b. Drizzle olive oil over the slices.
c. Bake for 20-25 minutes or until golden brown, flipping halfway through.

5. Layering:

a. In a baking dish, spread a thin layer of marinara sauce.

b. Arrange half of the baked eggplant slices over the sauce.

c. Sprinkle with mozzarella cheese and torn basil leaves.

d. Repeat the layers, finishing with a generous layer of mozzarella on top.

6. Bake Again:

Bake the assembled dish for an additional 25-30 minutes or until the cheese is melted and bubbly.

7. Serve:

Allow the Eggplant Parmesan to cool for a few minutes before serving. Garnish with fresh basil leaves.

Nutrition Information:

Note: Nutrition information may vary based on specific ingredients and portion sizes.

- Calories per serving: XXX
- Total Fat: XXg
- Saturated Fat: XXg
- Cholesterol: XXmg
- Sodium: XXXmg
- Total Carbohydrates: XXg
- Dietary Fiber: XXg
- Sugars: XXg
- Protein: XXg

Immerse yourself in the harmony of flavors as you savor the "Everything I Wanted Eggplant Parmesan," a dish that mirrors the audacious creativity of Billie Eilish.

11. No Time To Die Nachos

Get ready to dive into the world of Billie Eilish with a snack that's as bold and electrifying as her music—No Time To Die Nachos. Inspired by the intensity of the iconic James Bond theme, these nachos are loaded with flavors that pack a punch. Quick to make and impossible to resist, these nachos are perfect for when you need a snack in a hurry, just like the fast-paced beats of Billie's music.

Serving: Ideal for 4-6 people.

Preparation Time: 10 minutes
Ready Time: 15 minutes

Ingredients:
- 1 bag of tortilla chips
- 1 cup shredded cheddar cheese
- 1 cup diced tomatoes
- 1/2 cup diced red onions
- 1/2 cup sliced black olives
- 1/4 cup pickled jalapeños
- 1/2 cup sour cream
- 1/4 cup chopped fresh cilantro
- 1/2 cup guacamole

Instructions:
1. Preheat your oven to 350°F (175°C).
2. On a large oven-safe serving dish or baking sheet, spread out a layer of tortilla chips.
3. Sprinkle shredded cheddar cheese evenly over the chips.
4. Add diced tomatoes, red onions, black olives, and pickled jalapeños on top of the cheese.
5. Place the dish in the preheated oven and bake for about 10 minutes or until the cheese is melted and bubbly.
6. Remove from the oven and let it cool for a couple of minutes.
7. Drizzle dollops of sour cream over the nachos and garnish with chopped cilantro.
8. Spoon guacamole on top or serve it on the side.
9. Grab your favorite Billie Eilish playlist and enjoy these No Time To Die Nachos!

Nutrition Information:
Note: Nutritional values are approximate and may vary based on specific ingredients used.
- Calories per serving: 350
- Total fat: 22g
- Saturated fat: 9g
- Trans fat: 0g
- Cholesterol: 30mg
- Sodium: 600mg
- Total carbohydrates: 30g

- Dietary fiber: 5g
- Sugars: 3g
- Protein: 10g

Feel the rhythm, taste the excitement, and savor every moment with these No Time To Die Nachos. A culinary journey that echoes the vibrancy of Billie Eilish's music!

12. Your Power Yogurt Parfait

Embrace the bold and vibrant flavors with "Your Power Yogurt Parfait," a delightful creation inspired by the iconic Billie Eilish. This energizing parfait is a symphony of textures and tastes, reflecting the artist's dynamic style and creative spirit. Packed with wholesome ingredients, it's a treat that nourishes both body and soul. Get ready to indulge in a symphony of flavors that'll leave you feeling as empowered as Billie's music.

Serving: Serves 2
Preparation Time: 15 minutes
Ready Time: 15 minutes

Ingredients:
- 1 cup Greek yogurt
- 2 tablespoons honey
- 1 teaspoon vanilla extract
- 1 cup granola
- 1 cup mixed berries (strawberries, blueberries, raspberries)
- 1 ripe banana, sliced
- 1/4 cup chopped nuts (almonds, walnuts, or your choice)
- Fresh mint leaves for garnish

Instructions:
1. Prepare the Yogurt Base:
In a bowl, combine the Greek yogurt, honey, and vanilla extract. Mix well until smooth and creamy.
2. Layering:
- Start by adding a spoonful of the yogurt mixture to the bottom of each serving glass or bowl.

- Follow with a layer of granola, spreading it evenly.
- Add a layer of mixed berries, distributing them across the surface.
- Place sliced bananas on top, creating a visually appealing arrangement.
- Repeat the layers until the glass or bowl is filled.
3. Top it Off:
Finish with a generous sprinkle of chopped nuts for added crunch and a few fresh mint leaves for a burst of freshness.
4. Serve:
Chill the parfait in the refrigerator for at least 10 minutes before serving. When ready, present this vibrant creation and savor the harmony of flavors.

Nutrition Information:
Note: Nutrition values are approximate and may vary based on specific ingredients used.
- Calories: 350 per serving
- Protein: 15g
- Carbohydrates: 45g
- Dietary Fiber: 7g
- Sugars: 22g
- Fat: 12g
- Saturated Fat: 3g
- Cholesterol: 10mg
- Sodium: 60mg
Immerse yourself in the powerful combination of creamy yogurt, sweet honey, and the crunch of granola with "Your Power Yogurt Parfait." Inspired by Billie Eilish, this creation is not just a treat for your taste buds but a celebration of individuality and self-expression. Enjoy every spoonful and feel the empowerment!

13. Xanny X-shaped Pretzels

Embrace the twisty, eclectic world of Billie Eilish with these Xanny X-shaped Pretzels. Named after her hit song, these pretzels are as unique and bold as Billie herself. With a soft, doughy interior and a perfectly golden exterior, they're a delightful treat for any occasion.

Serving: Makes 8 pretzels

Preparation time: 30 minutes
Ready time: 1 hour 30 minutes

Ingredients:
- 1 ½ cups warm water (110-115°F)
- 1 tablespoon granulated sugar
- 2 ¼ teaspoons active dry yeast
- 4 cups all-purpose flour
- 1 teaspoon salt
- 1/3 cup baking soda
- 1 egg, beaten
- Coarse sea salt or pretzel salt, for sprinkling

Instructions:
1. In a bowl, combine the warm water and sugar. Sprinkle the yeast over the top and let it sit for 5-10 minutes until frothy.
2. In a large mixing bowl, combine the flour and salt. Pour in the activated yeast mixture and stir until a shaggy dough forms.
3. Knead the dough on a floured surface for about 5-7 minutes until it becomes smooth and elastic. Place the dough in a greased bowl, cover it with a clean kitchen towel, and let it rise in a warm place for about an hour or until doubled in size.
4. Preheat your oven to 450°F (230°C). Line a baking sheet with parchment paper.
5. Punch down the risen dough and divide it into 8 equal portions. Roll each portion into a long rope, about 18 inches in length. Shape the ropes into an "X" shape, crossing them in the center and twisting the ends around each other.
6. In a large pot, bring water to a boil and add the baking soda. Boil each pretzel for 30 seconds, then remove with a slotted spoon and place on the prepared baking sheet.
7. Brush the pretzels with beaten egg and sprinkle them with coarse sea salt or pretzel salt.
8. Bake for 10-12 minutes or until the pretzels turn golden brown.

Nutrition Information: *(per pretzel)*
* Calories: 230
* Total Fat: 1g
* Saturated Fat: 0g
* Cholesterol: 23mg

* Sodium: 1300mg
* Total Carbohydrate: 48g
* Dietary Fiber: 2g
* Sugars: 2g
* Protein: 7g

Enjoy these Xanny X-shaped Pretzels warm from the oven, perfect for munching on while you dive into the musical world of Billie Eilish!

14. NDA Nectarine Salad

Celebrate the vibrant spirit of Billie Eilish with the NDA Nectarine Salad—a melody of flavors that harmonize in every bite. Inspired by the artist's eclectic style, this refreshing salad captures the essence of her creativity and individuality. The combination of sweet nectarines, crisp greens, and a zesty vinaigrette will surely hit the right notes on your taste buds.

Serving: Serves 4
Preparation Time: 15 minutes
Ready Time: 15 minutes

Ingredients:
- 4 ripe nectarines, sliced
- 6 cups mixed salad greens
- 1 cup cherry tomatoes, halved
- 1/2 cup red onion, thinly sliced
- 1/2 cup feta cheese, crumbled
- 1/4 cup fresh basil leaves, torn
For the Vinaigrette:
- 3 tablespoons extra-virgin olive oil
- 2 tablespoons balsamic vinegar
- 1 teaspoon Dijon mustard
- 1 teaspoon honey
- Salt and pepper to taste

Instructions:
1. Prepare the Vinaigrette:

- In a small bowl, whisk together the olive oil, balsamic vinegar, Dijon mustard, honey, salt, and pepper. Set aside.
2. Assemble the Salad:
- In a large salad bowl, combine the mixed greens, sliced nectarines, cherry tomatoes, red onion, feta cheese, and torn basil leaves.
3. Drizzle with Vinaigrette:
- Pour the prepared vinaigrette over the salad ingredients. Toss gently to ensure an even coating.
4. Serve:
- Divide the NDA Nectarine Salad among four plates.
5. Garnish (Optional):
- Sprinkle additional feta cheese and basil leaves on top for a finishing touch.
6. Enjoy:
- Serve immediately and relish the symphony of flavors in this refreshing salad.

Nutrition Information:
(Per Serving)
- Calories: 220
- Protein: 4g
- Carbohydrates: 26g
- Fat: 12g
- Saturated Fat: 3.5g
- Cholesterol: 15mg
- Sodium: 280mg
- Fiber: 5g
- Sugar: 18g
Elevate your culinary experience with the NDA Nectarine Salad—an ode to Billie Eilish's distinctive style and a burst of freshness that will leave you craving an encore.

15. Therefore I Am Tofu Stir Fry

Billie Eilish, a musical sensation known for her unique style and bold creativity, has inspired us to create a dish that mirrors her individuality. "Therefore I Am Tofu Stir Fry" captures the essence of Billie's unapologetic spirit through a harmonious blend of flavors and textures.

This vegan stir fry is a celebration of self-expression, just like Billie's music.

Serving: 4 servings
Preparation Time: 15 minutes
Ready Time: 30 minutes

Ingredients:
- 1 block extra-firm tofu, pressed and cubed
- 2 tablespoons soy sauce
- 1 tablespoon sesame oil
- 1 tablespoon rice vinegar
- 1 tablespoon maple syrup
- 1 teaspoon cornstarch
- 2 tablespoons vegetable oil
- 1 red bell pepper, sliced
- 1 yellow bell pepper, sliced
- 1 cup broccoli florets
- 1 carrot, julienned
- 3 cloves garlic, minced
- 1 tablespoon ginger, minced
- 1 cup snow peas, ends trimmed
- 2 green onions, sliced
- Sesame seeds for garnish (optional)
- Cooked brown rice for serving

Instructions:
1. Prepare the Tofu:
- Press the tofu to remove excess water. Cut it into cubes.
- In a bowl, mix soy sauce, sesame oil, rice vinegar, maple syrup, and cornstarch to create the marinade.
- Toss the tofu cubes in the marinade and let them sit for at least 10 minutes.
2. Stir Fry:
- Heat vegetable oil in a large pan or wok over medium-high heat.
- Add marinated tofu cubes and cook until golden brown on all sides. Remove tofu from the pan and set aside.
3. Vegetable Medley:
- In the same pan, add a bit more oil if needed. Sauté garlic and ginger until fragrant.

- Add sliced bell peppers, broccoli, julienned carrot, and snow peas. Stir-fry until the vegetables are crisp-tender.
4. Combine and Finish:
- Return the cooked tofu to the pan with the vegetables.
- Toss everything together until well combined and heated through.
- Sprinkle sliced green onions and sesame seeds for garnish if desired.
5. Serve:
- Serve the Therefore I Am Tofu Stir Fry over cooked brown rice.

Nutrition Information (per serving):
- Calories: 320
- Total Fat: 18g
- Saturated Fat: 2g
- Trans Fat: 0g
- Cholesterol: 0mg
- Sodium: 680mg
- Total Carbohydrates: 28g
- Dietary Fiber: 6g
- Sugars: 10g
- Protein: 16g
Note: Nutrition information is approximate and may vary based on specific ingredients and serving sizes.

16. Lost Cause Lentil Soup

Get ready to experience the comforting embrace of the "Lost Cause Lentil Soup," a dish inspired by the soulful and rebellious spirit of Billie Eilish. This hearty lentil soup is a perfect blend of flavors, reflecting Billie's eclectic taste in music and style. Just like her music, this soup is a soothing yet bold composition that will warm your heart and satisfy your cravings.

Serving: 4-6 servings
Preparation Time: 15 minutes
Ready Time: 1 hour 15 minutes

Ingredients:
- 1 cup dried green or brown lentils, rinsed and drained

- 1 large onion, finely chopped
- 2 carrots, peeled and diced
- 2 celery stalks, diced
- 3 cloves garlic, minced
- 1 can (14 oz) diced tomatoes, undrained
- 6 cups vegetable broth
- 1 teaspoon ground cumin
- 1 teaspoon smoked paprika
- 1/2 teaspoon ground turmeric
- 1/2 teaspoon dried thyme
- Salt and pepper to taste
- 2 tablespoons olive oil
- Fresh parsley, chopped (for garnish)
- Lemon wedges (for serving)

Instructions:
1. In a large pot, heat olive oil over medium heat. Add chopped onions, carrots, and celery. Cook until vegetables are softened, about 5-7 minutes.
2. Add minced garlic and cook for an additional 1-2 minutes until fragrant.
3. Stir in lentils, diced tomatoes with their juice, vegetable broth, cumin, smoked paprika, turmeric, dried thyme, salt, and pepper.
4. Bring the soup to a boil, then reduce the heat to low, cover, and simmer for 1 hour or until lentils are tender.
5. Taste and adjust seasonings if necessary. If the soup is too thick, you can add more vegetable broth to reach your desired consistency.
6. Serve the Lost Cause Lentil Soup hot, garnished with fresh parsley and accompanied by lemon wedges for a bright burst of flavor.

Nutrition Information:
(Per Serving)
- Calories: 250
- Total Fat: 6g
- Saturated Fat: 1g
- Cholesterol: 0mg
- Sodium: 800mg
- Total Carbohydrates: 40g
- Dietary Fiber: 12g
- Sugars: 6g

- Protein: 12g

Indulge in this nourishing and soul-satisfying Lost Cause Lentil Soup as you immerse yourself in the essence of Billie Eilish's creativity. Each spoonful is a harmonious blend of ingredients that will leave you craving more of this musical-inspired culinary creation.

17. Happier Than Ever Hummus

Get ready to indulge in a musical and culinary journey with our "Happier Than Ever Hummus," inspired by the soulful vibes of Billie Eilish. This dish captures the essence of joy and satisfaction, mirroring the emotions evoked by Billie's iconic album, "Happier Than Ever." Dive into a delightful blend of flavors that will leave you humming with happiness.

Serving: Serves 4
Preparation Time: 15 minutes
Ready Time: 15 minutes

Ingredients:
- 2 cans (15 ounces each) chickpeas, drained and rinsed
- 1/3 cup tahini
- 2 cloves garlic, minced
- 1/4 cup extra-virgin olive oil, plus extra for drizzling
- Juice of 1 lemon
- 1 teaspoon ground cumin
- 1/2 teaspoon smoked paprika
- Salt and pepper to taste
- 2-3 tablespoons water (as needed for desired consistency)
- Fresh parsley, chopped, for garnish
- Optional toppings: Kalamata olives, cherry tomatoes, pine nuts

Instructions:
1. In a food processor, combine chickpeas, tahini, minced garlic, olive oil, lemon juice, ground cumin, smoked paprika, salt, and pepper.
2. Blend the ingredients until smooth, scraping down the sides as needed. If the hummus is too thick, add water, one tablespoon at a time, until the desired consistency is reached.

3. Taste and adjust seasoning as needed. If you prefer a stronger lemon flavor or more spice, feel free to customize to your liking.
4. Transfer the hummus to a serving bowl, creating a well in the center with the back of a spoon.
5. Drizzle extra-virgin olive oil over the top and sprinkle with chopped fresh parsley.
6. Garnish with your choice of optional toppings, such as Kalamata olives, cherry tomatoes, or pine nuts.
7. Serve the "Happier Than Ever Hummus" with pita bread, vegetable sticks, or your favorite crackers.

Nutrition Information:
(Per Serving)
- Calories: 250
- Total Fat: 15g
- Saturated Fat: 2g
- Cholesterol: 0mg
- Sodium: 350mg
- Total Carbohydrates: 25g
- Dietary Fiber: 7g
- Sugars: 3g
- Protein: 7g
Dive into this harmonious blend of flavors that will have you feeling "Happier Than Ever" with each savory bite. Enjoy the magic of music and food coming together in perfect harmony!

18. Oxytocin Orange Smoothie

Indulge your taste buds in the vibrant world of Billie Eilish with our Oxytocin Orange Smoothie. This refreshing blend is inspired by the artist's dynamic energy and zest for life. Packed with citrusy goodness and a hint of sweetness, this smoothie is a sensory experience that resonates with Billie's eclectic musical style. So, let the harmonious flavors of Oxytocin Orange Smoothie transport you to a melodious paradise!

Serving: 2 servings
Preparation Time: 10 minutes

Ready Time: 10 minutes

Ingredients:
- 2 large oranges, peeled and segmented
- 1 banana, peeled
- 1/2 cup Greek yogurt
- 1/2 cup almond milk
- 1 tablespoon honey
- 1/2 teaspoon vanilla extract
- Ice cubes (optional)
- Orange slices for garnish

Instructions:
1. Prepare the Ingredients:
Peel and segment the oranges. Peel the banana.
2. Blend the Fruits:
In a blender, combine the orange segments, banana, Greek yogurt, almond milk, honey, and vanilla extract. If you prefer a colder smoothie, add a handful of ice cubes.
3. Blend Until Smooth:
Blend the ingredients until smooth and creamy. Ensure that the consistency is to your liking.
4. Serve:
Pour the Oxytocin Orange Smoothie into glasses. Garnish with orange slices for an extra burst of citrusy freshness.
5. Enjoy:
Sip and savor the harmonious blend of flavors that make this smoothie a tribute to Billie Eilish's unique artistic expression.

Nutrition Information (per serving):
- Calories: 180
- Protein: 7g
- Fat: 3g
- Carbohydrates: 35g
- Fiber: 5g
- Sugar: 24g
- Vitamin C: 120% DV
- Calcium: 15% DV
- Iron: 2% DV

Note: Nutrition information is approximate and may vary based on specific ingredients used. Adjustments can be made based on dietary preferences and restrictions.

19. My Future Mango Salsa

Embrace the vibrant and eclectic flavors that echo the boldness of Billie Eilish with "My Future Mango Salsa." This lively salsa is a fusion of sweet and spicy, capturing the essence of Billie's dynamic musical style. Perfect for those who crave a melody of taste in every bite, this salsa is a celebration of individuality and creativity in the kitchen.

Serving: This recipe serves 4-6 people.
Preparation Time: 15 minutes
Ready Time: 30 minutes

Ingredients:
- 2 ripe mangoes, diced
- 1 cup cherry tomatoes, quartered
- 1/2 red onion, finely diced
- 1 jalapeño, seeded and finely chopped
- 1/4 cup fresh cilantro, chopped
- Juice of 2 limes
- 1 teaspoon honey
- Salt and pepper to taste

Instructions:
1. Prepare the Ingredients:
- Peel and dice the ripe mangoes.
- Quarter the cherry tomatoes.
- Finely dice the red onion.
- Seed and finely chop the jalapeño.
- Chop the fresh cilantro.
2. Combine the Ingredients:
- In a large mixing bowl, combine the diced mangoes, quartered cherry tomatoes, diced red onion, chopped jalapeño, and cilantro.
3. Create the Dressing:

- In a small bowl, whisk together the lime juice and honey until well combined.
4. Toss and Season:
- Pour the lime-honey dressing over the mango mixture.
- Gently toss everything together until well combined.
- Season with salt and pepper to taste.
5. Chill:
- Allow the salsa to chill in the refrigerator for at least 15 minutes to let the flavors meld.
6. Serve:
- Once chilled, give the salsa a final stir and serve it with tortilla chips, grilled chicken, or as a refreshing side dish.

Nutrition Information:
Note: Nutrition information is approximate and may vary based on specific ingredients used.
- Calories: 80 per serving
- Total Fat: 0.5g
- Saturated Fat: 0g
- Cholesterol: 0mg
- Sodium: 5mg
- Total Carbohydrates: 20g
- Dietary Fiber: 2g
- Sugars: 16g
- Protein: 1g
Dive into the harmonious blend of sweet mangoes, zesty lime, and the kick of jalapeño with "My Future Mango Salsa," a culinary creation inspired by the spirit of Billie Eilish.

20. Getting Older Gingerbread Cookies

As Billie Eilish continues to captivate the world with her soulful tunes and unique style, we bring you a delightful recipe inspired by her creativity and individuality. These "Getting Older Gingerbread Cookies" not only pay homage to Billie's hit song but also offer a comforting and flavorful treat perfect for the holiday season. Dive into the world of Billie Eilish with each bite of these spiced and tender gingerbread cookies.

Serving: Makes approximately 24 cookies.
Preparation Time: 15 minutes.
Ready Time: 1 hour 30 minutes.

Ingredients:
- 3 cups all-purpose flour
- 1 teaspoon baking soda
- 1/4 teaspoon salt
- 1 tablespoon ground ginger
- 1 tablespoon ground cinnamon
- 1/2 teaspoon ground cloves
- 1/2 teaspoon ground nutmeg
- 3/4 cup unsalted butter, softened
- 3/4 cup brown sugar, packed
- 1/2 cup molasses
- 1 large egg
- 1 teaspoon vanilla extract

Instructions:
1. In a medium bowl, whisk together the flour, baking soda, salt, ginger, cinnamon, cloves, and nutmeg. Set aside.
2. In a large mixing bowl, cream together the softened butter and brown sugar until light and fluffy.
3. Add the molasses, egg, and vanilla extract to the butter mixture. Mix until well combined.
4. Gradually add the dry ingredients to the wet ingredients, mixing just until the dough comes together. Be careful not to overmix.
5. Divide the dough in half, shape each half into a disc, wrap in plastic wrap, and refrigerate for at least 1 hour.
6. Preheat the oven to 350°F (180°C) and line baking sheets with parchment paper.
7. On a lightly floured surface, roll out the chilled dough to about 1/4-inch thickness. Use gingerbread-shaped cookie cutters to cut out cookies and place them on the prepared baking sheets.
8. Bake for 8-10 minutes or until the edges are set. Allow the cookies to cool on the baking sheets for a few minutes before transferring them to a wire rack to cool completely.
9. Once cooled, you can decorate the cookies with icing or enjoy them as is.

Nutrition Information:
Per Serving (1 cookie):
- Calories: 120
- Total Fat: 5g
- Saturated Fat: 3g
- Cholesterol: 18mg
- Sodium: 65mg
- Total Carbohydrates: 18g
- Dietary Fiber: 0.5g
- Sugars: 8g
- Protein: 1g
Note: Nutrition Information is approximate and may vary based on specific ingredients used.

21. Halley's Comet Haddock Tacos

Inspired by the cosmic vibes of Billie Eilish, these Halley's Comet Haddock Tacos are a celestial delight for your taste buds. Named after the legendary comet, these tacos are a fusion of flavors that will transport you to another dimension. Get ready to embark on a flavor journey that's as unique and extraordinary as Billie's music.

Serving: 4 tacos
Preparation Time: 20 minutes
Ready Time: 30 minutes

Ingredients:
- 1 pound fresh haddock fillets
- 4 small tortillas (corn or flour)
- 1 cup purple cabbage, shredded
- 1 large avocado, sliced
- 1/2 cup cherry tomatoes, halved
- 1/4 cup red onion, finely chopped
- 1/4 cup fresh cilantro, chopped
- 1 lime, cut into wedges
For the Haddock Marinade:
- 2 tablespoons olive oil
- 1 tablespoon lime juice

- 1 teaspoon ground cumin
- 1 teaspoon chili powder
- 1/2 teaspoon garlic powder
- Salt and pepper to taste
For the Sauce:
- 1/2 cup plain Greek yogurt
- 1 tablespoon mayonnaise
- 1 tablespoon lime juice
- 1 teaspoon honey
- Salt to taste

Instructions:
1. Marinate the Haddock:
- In a bowl, mix olive oil, lime juice, cumin, chili powder, garlic powder, salt, and pepper.
- Coat haddock fillets with the marinade and let them marinate for at least 15 minutes.
2. Prepare the Sauce:
- In a small bowl, combine Greek yogurt, mayonnaise, lime juice, honey, and a pinch of salt. Mix well and set aside.
3. Cook the Haddock:
- Heat a skillet over medium heat.
- Cook the marinated haddock fillets for 3-4 minutes per side or until they are cooked through and easily flake with a fork.
4. Assemble the Tacos:
- Warm the tortillas in the skillet or microwave.
- Place a haddock fillet on each tortilla.
- Top with shredded purple cabbage, avocado slices, cherry tomatoes, red onion, and fresh cilantro.
5. Drizzle with Sauce:
- Drizzle the prepared sauce over the taco filling.
6. Serve:
- Serve the Halley's Comet Haddock Tacos with lime wedges on the side.

Nutrition Information (per serving):
Note: Nutrition values are approximate and may vary depending on specific ingredients used.
- Calories: 350
- Protein: 25g
- Fat: 15g

- Carbohydrates: 30g
- Fiber: 6g
- Sugar: 5g
- Sodium: 450mg

Embark on a cosmic culinary adventure with these Halley's Comet Haddock Tacos, and let the flavors take you to the stars!

22. I Love You Ice Cream Cone

Get ready to indulge in the sweet symphony of flavors with the "I Love You Ice Cream Cone," a delectable creation inspired by the enchanting world of Billie Eilish. This whimsical treat combines the joy of ice cream with a touch of romance, making it the perfect dessert to celebrate the magic in everyday moments. Treat yourself and your loved ones to this delightful concoction that's as unique and extraordinary as Billie's musical artistry.

Serving: 4 servings
Preparation Time: 15 minutes
Ready Time: 4 hours (including freezing time)

Ingredients:
- 4 sugar cones
- 2 cups vanilla ice cream
- 1/2 cup chocolate chips, melted
- 1/4 cup heart-shaped sprinkles
- 4 maraschino cherries (optional, for garnish)

Instructions:
1. Prepare the Cones:
- Take the sugar cones and gently melt the edges by running them over a warm stove or dipping them in melted chocolate. This step adds a touch of decadence to your cones.
2. Fill with Love:
- Allow the melted chocolate to cool for a moment, then dip the rim of each cone into the melted chocolate, followed by the heart-shaped sprinkles. Set aside to let the chocolate set.
3. Chill Out:

- Scoop the vanilla ice cream into each cone, creating a generous swirl at the top. Ensure the ice cream is packed tightly to avoid any air gaps.
4. Drizzle the Love:
- Drizzle the remaining melted chocolate over the top of the ice cream swirls, letting it cascade down the sides for an artistic touch.
5. Freeze and Set:
- Place the cones in the freezer for at least 4 hours, allowing the ice cream and chocolate to firm up.
6. Final Flourish:
- Before serving, garnish each cone with a maraschino cherry for that extra pop of color and flavor.

Nutrition Information:
(Per Serving)
- Calories: 320
- Fat: 15g
- Saturated Fat: 9g
- Cholesterol: 45mg
- Sodium: 90mg
- Carbohydrates: 45g
- Fiber: 2g
- Sugar: 30g
- Protein: 4g

Indulge in the "I Love You Ice Cream Cone" and savor the delightful combination of textures and flavors that mirror the extraordinary essence of Billie Eilish's creativity. Enjoy this sweet symphony and let it serenade your taste buds with every joyful bite!

23. Not My Responsibility Noodle Bowl

Indulge your taste buds in a symphony of flavors with the "Not My Responsibility Noodle Bowl," a dish inspired by the unapologetic creativity of Billie Eilish. Just like Billie's music, this noodle bowl is a fusion of bold and unexpected elements that come together in perfect harmony. With a mix of textures and tastes, this dish is a culinary representation of breaking free from expectations and embracing individuality.

Serving: 4 servings
Preparation Time: 15 minutes
Ready Time: 30 minutes

Ingredients:
- 8 oz rice noodles
- 1 lb shrimp, peeled and deveined
- 2 cups broccoli florets
- 1 red bell pepper, thinly sliced
- 1 carrot, julienned
- 3 cloves garlic, minced
- 1 tablespoon fresh ginger, grated
- 1/4 cup soy sauce
- 2 tablespoons oyster sauce
- 1 tablespoon sesame oil
- 1 tablespoon rice vinegar
- 1 tablespoon brown sugar
- 2 tablespoons vegetable oil
- 2 green onions, thinly sliced (for garnish)
- Sesame seeds (for garnish)

Instructions:
1. Prepare the Rice Noodles:
- Cook the rice noodles according to the package instructions. Drain and set aside.
2. Sauté Shrimp:
- In a large skillet, heat 1 tablespoon of vegetable oil over medium-high heat.
- Add the shrimp and cook until pink and opaque, about 2-3 minutes per side. Remove shrimp from the skillet and set aside.
3. Vegetable Medley:
- In the same skillet, add another tablespoon of vegetable oil.
- Sauté garlic and ginger until fragrant.
- Add broccoli, bell pepper, and carrot. Cook until the vegetables are tender-crisp.
4. Create the Sauce:
- In a small bowl, whisk together soy sauce, oyster sauce, sesame oil, rice vinegar, and brown sugar.
- Pour the sauce over the vegetables in the skillet and stir to coat evenly.
5. Combine and Serve:

- Add the cooked rice noodles and sautéed shrimp to the skillet.
- Toss everything together until well combined and heated through.
6. Garnish:
- Serve the noodle bowl hot, garnished with sliced green onions and sesame seeds.

Nutrition Information:
(Per Serving)
- Calories: 450 kcal
- Protein: 25g
- Carbohydrates: 60g
- Fat: 12g
- Fiber: 5g
- Sugar: 7g
Savor the "Not My Responsibility Noodle Bowl" as a tribute to Billie Eilish's fearless spirit and enjoy a dish that's as unique as you are.

24. Overheated Oatmeal Cookies

Indulge in the rebellious spirit of Billie Eilish with these "Overheated Oatmeal Cookies." Inspired by the fiery energy of Billie's music, these cookies are a fusion of wholesome oats and intense flavors that will leave your taste buds craving more. Get ready to experience a symphony of textures and tastes that echo Billie's eclectic style.

Serving: Makes approximately 24 cookies
Preparation Time: 15 minutes
Ready Time: 30 minutes

Ingredients:
- 1 cup unsalted butter, softened
- 1 cup brown sugar, packed
- 1/2 cup granulated sugar
- 2 large eggs
- 1 teaspoon vanilla extract
- 1 1/2 cups all-purpose flour
- 1 teaspoon baking soda
- 1/2 teaspoon salt

- 3 cups old-fashioned oats
- 1 cup dark chocolate chunks
- 1/2 cup chopped walnuts or pecans (optional)

Instructions:
1. Preheat your oven to 350°F (175°C) and line a baking sheet with parchment paper.
2. In a large mixing bowl, cream together the softened butter, brown sugar, and granulated sugar until light and fluffy.
3. Add the eggs one at a time, beating well after each addition. Stir in the vanilla extract.
4. In a separate bowl, whisk together the flour, baking soda, and salt.
5. Gradually add the dry ingredients to the wet ingredients, mixing until just combined.
6. Fold in the oats, dark chocolate chunks, and nuts (if using) until evenly distributed throughout the cookie dough.
7. Drop rounded tablespoons of dough onto the prepared baking sheet, spacing them about 2 inches apart.
8. Bake in the preheated oven for 10-12 minutes or until the edges are golden brown. The centers may still look slightly undercooked but will firm up as they cool.
9. Allow the cookies to cool on the baking sheet for 5 minutes before transferring them to a wire rack to cool completely.
10. Once cooled, serve and enjoy the overheated goodness of these oatmeal cookies.

Nutrition Information:
Note: Nutrition information is approximate and may vary based on specific ingredients used.
- Calories per serving: 180
- Total Fat: 10g
- Saturated Fat: 6g
- Cholesterol: 35mg
- Sodium: 120mg
- Total Carbohydrates: 22g
- Dietary Fiber: 2g
- Sugars: 11g
- Protein: 3g

Indulge in these Overheated Oatmeal Cookies as a sweet homage to the bold and vibrant spirit of Billie Eilish. Each bite is a celebration of flavor, texture, and the unique inspiration behind this delectable treat.

25. Male Fantasy Mango Sorbet

Indulge in the enchanting world of Billie Eilish-inspired cuisine with our "Male Fantasy Mango Sorbet." This delectable treat pays homage to Billie's ethereal musical realm and her hit song "Male Fantasy." Immerse yourself in the rich flavors of ripe mangoes, creating a sorbet that's as bold and sweet as Billie's iconic style.

Serving: Serves 4
Preparation Time: 15 minutes
Ready Time: 4 hours (including freezing time)

Ingredients:
- 4 cups ripe mango, peeled and diced
- 1 cup granulated sugar
- 1/2 cup water
- 2 tablespoons fresh lime juice
- 1 teaspoon lime zest
- Pinch of salt

Instructions:
1. In a small saucepan, combine sugar and water over medium heat. Stir until the sugar dissolves completely, creating a simple syrup. Remove from heat and let it cool to room temperature.
2. In a blender, combine the diced mangoes, lime juice, lime zest, and a pinch of salt. Blend until smooth and creamy.
3. Slowly add the cooled simple syrup to the mango mixture, blending continuously until well combined.
4. Pour the sorbet mixture into an ice cream maker and churn according to the manufacturer's instructions until it reaches a soft-serve consistency.
5. Transfer the sorbet to a lidded container and freeze for at least 4 hours or until firm.

6. Before serving, let the sorbet sit at room temperature for a few minutes to soften slightly. Scoop into bowls or cones, and garnish with additional lime zest if desired.

Nutrition Information:
(Per Serving)
- Calories: 180
- Total Fat: 0g
- Cholesterol: 0mg
- Sodium: 1mg
- Total Carbohydrates: 46g
- Dietary Fiber: 2g
- Sugars: 42g
- Protein: 1g

Immerse yourself in the dreamy notes of Billie Eilish's music while savoring the tropical allure of this Male Fantasy Mango Sorbet. A tantalizing symphony of flavors awaits, capturing the essence of Billie's artistry in every refreshing bite.

26. Oxytocin Oat Pancakes

Indulge in the rhythmic symphony of flavors with our "Oxytocin Oat Pancakes," a culinary creation inspired by the eclectic and soulful vibes of Billie Eilish. Just like Billie's music, these pancakes are a harmonious blend of wholesome ingredients that will set the tone for a delightful breakfast experience. Packed with oats and a touch of sweetness, these pancakes will surely hit all the right notes on your taste buds.

Serving: This recipe makes approximately 8 pancakes.
Preparation Time: 15 minutes
Ready Time: 30 minutes

Ingredients:
- 1 cup rolled oats
- 1 cup all-purpose flour
- 2 tablespoons brown sugar
- 1 teaspoon baking powder
- 1/2 teaspoon baking soda

- 1/4 teaspoon salt
- 1 cup buttermilk
- 1/2 cup milk
- 2 large eggs
- 2 tablespoons melted butter
- 1 teaspoon vanilla extract
- 1/4 cup dark chocolate chips (optional)
- Cooking spray or additional butter for greasing the pan

Instructions:
1. In a blender or food processor, pulse the rolled oats until they form a coarse flour-like consistency.
2. In a large mixing bowl, combine the oat flour, all-purpose flour, brown sugar, baking powder, baking soda, and salt.
3. In a separate bowl, whisk together the buttermilk, milk, eggs, melted butter, and vanilla extract.
4. Pour the wet ingredients into the dry ingredients and stir until just combined. Be careful not to overmix; a few lumps are okay.
5. If desired, fold in the dark chocolate chips for an extra touch of indulgence.
6. Heat a griddle or non-stick pan over medium heat and lightly coat with cooking spray or butter.
7. Pour 1/4 cup portions of batter onto the griddle for each pancake. Cook until bubbles form on the surface, then flip and cook until golden brown on the other side.
8. Repeat until all the batter is used, keeping the cooked pancakes warm in a low oven if necessary.
9. Serve the Oxytocin Oat Pancakes with your favorite toppings, such as fresh berries, maple syrup, or a dollop of whipped cream.

Nutrition Information:
(Per Serving - 2 pancakes)
- Calories: 250
- Total Fat: 9g
- Saturated Fat: 5g
- Cholesterol: 70mg
- Sodium: 350mg
- Total Carbohydrates: 35g
- Dietary Fiber: 2g
- Sugars: 8g

- Protein: 7g

Feel the warmth of these pancakes as they bring a sense of comfort and joy to your breakfast table – just like the music of Billie Eilish. Enjoy!

27. Your Power Yellow Pepper Soup

Get ready to experience the vibrant flavors that echo the energy and creativity of Billie Eilish with "Your Power Yellow Pepper Soup." This soup is as bold and unique as Billie herself, combining the warmth of yellow peppers with a kick of spice to create a symphony of flavors that will leave your taste buds dancing.

Serving: 4 servings
Preparation Time: 15 minutes
Ready Time: 40 minutes

Ingredients:
- 4 large yellow bell peppers, roasted and peeled
- 1 tablespoon olive oil
- 1 onion, diced
- 3 cloves garlic, minced
- 1 teaspoon ground cumin
- 1 teaspoon smoked paprika
- 1/2 teaspoon cayenne pepper (adjust to taste)
- 4 cups vegetable broth
- 1 can (15 ounces) chickpeas, drained and rinsed
- Salt and pepper to taste
- Fresh cilantro for garnish
- Optional: a squeeze of lime juice for extra brightness

Instructions:
1. Roast the Peppers:
- Preheat the oven broiler. Place the yellow peppers on a baking sheet and broil, turning occasionally until the skin is charred and blistered. Transfer the peppers to a bowl, cover with plastic wrap, and let them steam for 10 minutes. Peel off the skin, remove the seeds, and chop the flesh.
2. Sauté Aromatics:

- In a large pot, heat the olive oil over medium heat. Add the diced onion and sauté until translucent. Add minced garlic and sauté for an additional minute until fragrant.
3. Spice it Up:
- Stir in the ground cumin, smoked paprika, and cayenne pepper, allowing the spices to toast for about a minute.
4. Simmer the Soup:
- Add the roasted yellow peppers, vegetable broth, and chickpeas to the pot. Bring the mixture to a boil, then reduce the heat and let it simmer for 20-25 minutes to allow the flavors to meld.
5. Blend to Perfection:
- Use an immersion blender to puree the soup until smooth. Alternatively, transfer the soup in batches to a blender, being careful not to overfill, and blend until smooth.
6. Season and Serve:
- Season the soup with salt and pepper to taste. Ladle into bowls and garnish with fresh cilantro. Add a squeeze of lime juice if desired for an extra burst of flavor.

Nutrition Information:
Note: Nutritional values are approximate and may vary based on specific ingredients and serving sizes.
- Calories: 180 per serving
- Protein: 5g
- Carbohydrates: 30g
- Fiber: 7g
- Fat: 6g
- Saturated Fat: 1g
- Cholesterol: 0mg
- Sodium: 800mg
- Potassium: 550mg
- Vitamin A: 60%
- Vitamin C: 240%
- Calcium: 6%
- Iron: 15%
Get ready to savor the bold and empowering flavors of "Your Power Yellow Pepper Soup," a dish inspired by the creativity and spirit of Billie Eilish.

28. My Strange Addiction Mushroom Risotto

Indulge your taste buds in a symphony of flavors with the "My Strange Addiction Mushroom Risotto," a culinary creation inspired by the eclectic and unique style of Billie Eilish. This dish promises to take your palate on a journey as captivating as the artist herself. With the earthiness of mushrooms and the creamy richness of risotto, this recipe is a harmonious blend of unconventional ingredients that mirror Billie's distinct musical style.

Serving: 4 servings
Preparation Time: 15 minutes
Ready Time: 40 minutes

Ingredients:
- 1 1/2 cups Arborio rice
- 4 cups chicken or vegetable broth (warmed)
- 1 cup dry white wine
- 1 onion, finely chopped
- 2 cloves garlic, minced
- 1 cup assorted mushrooms (shiitake, cremini, oyster), sliced
- 1/2 cup dried porcini mushrooms, rehydrated in hot water and chopped
- 1/2 cup Parmesan cheese, grated
- 1/4 cup unsalted butter
- 2 tablespoons olive oil
- Salt and pepper to taste
- Fresh parsley, chopped (for garnish)

Instructions:
1. In a large pan, heat the olive oil and 1 tablespoon of butter over medium heat. Add the chopped onion and garlic, sautéing until they become translucent.
2. Stir in the Arborio rice, ensuring each grain is coated with the butter and oil mixture. Cook for 2-3 minutes until the rice becomes lightly toasted.
3. Pour in the white wine, allowing it to simmer until mostly absorbed by the rice.

4. Begin adding the warm broth, one ladle at a time, stirring frequently. Allow the liquid to be absorbed before adding the next ladle. Continue this process until the rice is creamy and cooked to al dente texture.

5. In a separate pan, sauté the assorted mushrooms, including the rehydrated porcini, until they release their moisture and become golden brown.

6. Fold the sautéed mushrooms into the risotto, along with the remaining butter and grated Parmesan cheese. Season with salt and pepper to taste.

7. Once everything is well combined and the risotto reaches a creamy consistency, remove it from the heat.

8. Serve the My Strange Addiction Mushroom Risotto hot, garnished with chopped fresh parsley.

Nutrition Information:
(Per Serving)
- Calories: 450
- Fat: 18g
- Saturated Fat: 9g
- Cholesterol: 40mg
- Sodium: 800mg
- Carbohydrates: 55g
- Fiber: 3g
- Sugars: 2g
- Protein: 12g

Experience the allure of this dish that pays homage to Billie Eilish's unconventional charm – My Strange Addiction Mushroom Risotto will be a hit for both your taste buds and your soul.

29. All The Good Girls Go To Hell Grapefruit Salad

Indulge your taste buds with a culinary journey inspired by the iconic Billie Eilish. This cookbook features 98 food ideas that capture the essence of her music and style. One such creation is the "All The Good Girls Go To Hell Grapefruit Salad." This refreshing and vibrant dish mirrors the bold and eclectic spirit of Billie's music. Packed with flavors that pop, this salad is a delightful ode to the rebellious side in all of us.

Serving: 4 servings

Preparation Time: 15 minutes
Ready Time: 20 minutes

Ingredients:
- 2 large grapefruits, segmented
- 1 avocado, sliced
- 1 cup cherry tomatoes, halved
- 1/2 red onion, thinly sliced
- 1/4 cup fresh mint leaves, chopped
- 1/4 cup feta cheese, crumbled
- 1/4 cup chopped pistachios
- 2 tablespoons extra-virgin olive oil
- 1 tablespoon balsamic vinegar
- Salt and pepper to taste

Instructions:
1. Prepare the Ingredients: Start by segmenting the grapefruits, slicing the avocado, halving the cherry tomatoes, and thinly slicing the red onion. Chop the fresh mint leaves, crumble the feta cheese, and chop the pistachios.
2. Assemble the Salad: In a large salad bowl, combine the grapefruit segments, avocado slices, halved cherry tomatoes, sliced red onion, chopped mint leaves, crumbled feta cheese, and chopped pistachios.
3. Dress the Salad: Drizzle the extra-virgin olive oil and balsamic vinegar over the salad. Gently toss the ingredients to ensure an even coating. Season with salt and pepper to taste.
4. Serve: Divide the salad into individual serving plates or bowls.
5. Garnish: Sprinkle additional feta cheese and pistachios on top for an extra burst of flavor and texture.
6. Enjoy: This salad is best enjoyed immediately for maximum freshness and flavor.

Nutrition Information:
(Per Serving)
- Calories: 220
- Total Fat: 15g
- Saturated Fat: 4g
- Cholesterol: 15mg
- Sodium: 200mg
- Total Carbohydrates: 20g

- Dietary Fiber: 6g
- Sugars: 10g
- Protein: 5g

Dive into the vibrant world of Billie Eilish with this "All The Good Girls Go To Hell Grapefruit Salad." It's a harmonious blend of flavors and textures that will leave your taste buds singing.

30. Your Power Yellow Curry

Indulge in the vibrant and electrifying flavors of "Your Power Yellow Curry," a culinary creation inspired by the sensational Billie Eilish. This dish reflects the boldness and creativity that defines Billie's music, offering a symphony of aromatic spices and wholesome ingredients that come together in a harmonious fusion. Let this curry be a manifestation of your culinary power and a celebration of individuality.

Serving: 4 servings
Preparation Time: 15 minutes
Ready Time: 45 minutes

Ingredients:
- 1 lb (450g) boneless, skinless chicken thighs, cut into bite-sized pieces
- 2 tablespoons yellow curry paste
- 1 can (14 oz/400ml) coconut milk
- 1 large potato, peeled and diced
- 1 large carrot, sliced
- 1 bell pepper, thinly sliced
- 1 onion, finely chopped
- 2 cloves garlic, minced
- 1 tablespoon ginger, grated
- 2 tablespoons vegetable oil
- 1 tablespoon fish sauce (optional for non-vegetarian version)
- 1 tablespoon soy sauce
- 1 tablespoon brown sugar
- 1 lime, juiced
- Fresh cilantro, for garnish
- Cooked jasmine rice, for serving

Instructions:
1. In a large pot or deep skillet, heat vegetable oil over medium heat. Add chopped onion, minced garlic, and grated ginger. Sauté until the onion becomes translucent.
2. Add yellow curry paste to the pot and stir well, allowing the spices to release their flavors. Cook for 2-3 minutes until fragrant.
3. Add chicken pieces to the pot and cook until they are browned on all sides.
4. Pour in the coconut milk, stirring to combine with the curry paste and chicken. Bring the mixture to a gentle simmer.
5. Add diced potatoes, sliced carrots, and bell pepper to the pot. If you're preparing the non-vegetarian version, add fish sauce at this stage for an extra depth of flavor.
6. Season the curry with soy sauce, brown sugar, and lime juice. Stir well and let the curry simmer for 25-30 minutes or until the vegetables are tender and the chicken is fully cooked.
7. Adjust seasoning to taste. If you prefer a spicier curry, you can add more curry paste.
8. Serve the yellow curry over a bed of jasmine rice. Garnish with fresh cilantro for a burst of color and added freshness.

Nutrition Information (per serving):
Note: Nutrition information may vary based on specific ingredients and quantities used.
- Calories: 450
- Protein: 25g
- Fat: 30g
- Carbohydrates: 20g
- Fiber: 3g
- Sugar: 6g
- Sodium: 800mg

Dive into the bold flavors of "Your Power Yellow Curry" and savor the unique blend of ingredients that pay homage to the creativity of Billie Eilish. This dish is a testament to the power of individual expression and culinary exploration.

31. Goldwing Goldfish Crackers

Dive into the whimsical world of Billie Eilish with the "Goldwing Goldfish Crackers." Inspired by Billie's unique style and creativity, these golden-hued, bite-sized crackers are as playful and bold as her music. Whether you're hosting a Billie Eilish-themed party or simply want to add a touch of glam to your snack game, these crackers are sure to make a statement. Get ready to snack like a rockstar!

Serving: Serves 4-6
Preparation Time: 15 minutes
Ready Time: 30 minutes

Ingredients:
- 2 cups goldfish-shaped crackers
- 1/4 cup unsalted butter, melted
- 1 tablespoon honey
- 1 teaspoon edible gold dust (available at baking supply stores)
- 1/2 teaspoon sea salt (optional, for a sweet-savory balance)

Instructions:
1. Preheat your oven to 275°F (135°C).
2. In a large mixing bowl, combine the goldfish-shaped crackers with melted butter, ensuring each piece is evenly coated.
3. Drizzle honey over the crackers, stirring gently to distribute it evenly.
4. Spread the coated crackers in a single layer on a baking sheet lined with parchment paper.
5. Bake in the preheated oven for 15-20 minutes or until the crackers are golden and slightly crispy.
6. Remove from the oven and let them cool for a few minutes.
7. While the crackers are still warm, sprinkle edible gold dust over them. This will give them a glamorous, golden shine.
8. If you prefer a sweet-savory flavor, sprinkle a pinch of sea salt over the crackers.
9. Allow the Goldwing Goldfish Crackers to cool completely before serving.

Nutrition Information:
(Per Serving)
- Calories: 180
- Total Fat: 10g
- Saturated Fat: 5g

- Trans Fat: 0g
- Cholesterol: 20mg
- Sodium: 250mg
- Total Carbohydrates: 20g
- Dietary Fiber: 1g
- Sugars: 5g
- Protein: 3g

Note: Nutrition information is approximate and may vary based on specific ingredients used.

Now, indulge in the glimmering goodness of Goldwing Goldfish Crackers and let the music of Billie Eilish elevate your snacking experience!

32. Everybody Dies Golden Apple Pie

'Everybody Dies Golden Apple Pie" is a delectable dessert inspired by the eclectic and thought-provoking music of Billie Eilish. This golden-hued apple pie pays homage to her hit song "Everybody Dies" and captures the essence of the song's emotional depth in a delicious, comforting treat. With a crisp, buttery crust and a luscious apple filling, this pie is sure to be a hit at any gathering, just like Billie Eilish's chart-topping hits.

Serving: 8 servings
Preparation Time: 20 minutes
Ready Time: 1 hour 30 minutes

Ingredients:
- 6 cups thinly sliced, peeled apples (a mix of tart and sweet varieties)
- 3/4 cup granulated sugar
- 2 tablespoons all-purpose flour
- 1 teaspoon ground cinnamon
- 1/4 teaspoon ground nutmeg
- 1/4 teaspoon salt
- 1 tablespoon lemon juice
- 1 package (14 ounces) refrigerated pie crusts (or homemade if preferred)
- 2 tablespoons unsalted butter, cut into small pieces

- 1 egg, beaten (for egg wash)
- 1 tablespoon turbinado sugar (for sprinkling)

Instructions:

1. Preheat the Oven:

Preheat your oven to 425°F (220°C).

2. Prepare the Apples:

In a large bowl, combine the sliced apples, granulated sugar, flour, cinnamon, nutmeg, salt, and lemon juice. Toss until the apples are evenly coated, and set aside.

3. Roll Out the Pie Crusts:

Roll out one pie crust and place it into a 9-inch pie dish. Leave any excess hanging over the edges. Roll out the second crust on a lightly floured surface.

4. Fill the Pie:

Transfer the apple filling into the pie crust in the dish. Dot the top of the filling with small pieces of butter.

5. Top with Second Crust:

Place the second rolled-out crust over the apple filling. Trim the excess edges, leaving a little overhang. Press the edges of the top and bottom crusts together to seal. Crimp the edges with a fork or your fingers.

6. Vent the Pie:

Cut a few slits in the top crust to allow steam to escape during baking.

7. Egg Wash and Sugar:

Brush the top crust with beaten egg and sprinkle turbinado sugar over it for a golden, crunchy finish.

8. Bake:

Place the pie on a baking sheet to catch any drips and bake in the preheated oven for 45-50 minutes or until the crust is golden brown and the filling is bubbly.

9. Cool:

Allow the pie to cool on a wire rack for at least 1 hour before serving.

Nutrition Information:

(Per serving)
- Calories: 320
- Total Fat: 13g
- Saturated Fat: 6g
- Trans Fat: 0g
- Cholesterol: 30mg

- Sodium: 280mg
- Total Carbohydrates: 50g
- Dietary Fiber: 3g
- Sugars: 28g
- Protein: 2g

Enjoy the "Everybody Dies Golden Apple Pie" with a scoop of vanilla ice cream or a dollop of whipped cream for a truly sensational dessert experience inspired by the music of Billie Eilish!

33. Exile Espresso Brownies

Indulge your taste buds in the rebellious symphony of flavors with these Exile Espresso Brownies inspired by the bold and eclectic style of Billie Eilish. Rich, decadent, and infused with the essence of espresso, these brownies are a harmonious blend of sweetness and intensity. Let the vibrant spirit of Billie Eilish guide you through the creation of this rebelliously delicious treat!

Serving: Makes 16 brownies
Preparation Time: 15 minutes
Ready Time: 45 minutes

Ingredients:
- 1 cup (2 sticks) unsalted butter, melted
- 2 cups granulated sugar
- 1 cup all-purpose flour
- 1 cup unsweetened cocoa powder
- 4 large eggs
- 1 tablespoon vanilla extract
- 1/2 teaspoon salt
- 2 tablespoons finely ground espresso beans
- 1 cup chocolate chips (dark or semi-sweet)

Instructions:
1. Preheat your oven to 350°F (175°C). Grease a 9x9-inch baking pan and line it with parchment paper, leaving an overhang on two opposite sides for easy removal.

2. In a large mixing bowl, combine the melted butter and sugar. Stir until well combined.

3. Add the eggs one at a time, beating well after each addition. Mix in the vanilla extract.

4. In a separate bowl, whisk together the flour, cocoa powder, and salt. Gradually add the dry ingredients to the wet ingredients, mixing until just combined.

5. Gently fold in the finely ground espresso beans and chocolate chips, ensuring an even distribution throughout the batter.

6. Pour the batter into the prepared baking pan and smooth the top with a spatula.

7. Bake in the preheated oven for 30-35 minutes or until a toothpick inserted into the center comes out with moist crumbs (not wet batter).

8. Allow the brownies to cool in the pan for 10 minutes, then use the parchment paper overhang to lift them onto a wire rack to cool completely.

9. Once cooled, cut into 16 squares and serve with a dusting of cocoa powder or a dollop of whipped cream for an extra treat.

Nutrition Information:
(Per serving, based on 16 servings)
- Calories: 280
- Total Fat: 16g
- Saturated Fat: 9g
- Trans Fat: 0g
- Cholesterol: 80mg
- Sodium: 90mg
- Total Carbohydrates: 34g
- Dietary Fiber: 3g
- Sugars: 24g
- Protein: 4g
Note: Nutrition values are approximate and may vary based on specific ingredients used.

34. All The Good Girls Go To Hell Guava Smoothie

Indulge in the rebellious flavors of Billie Eilish's music with the "All The Good Girls Go To Hell Guava Smoothie." This vibrant and energizing smoothie pays homage to Billie's hit song while offering a sweet escape for your taste buds. Packed with the goodness of guava and a hint of attitude, this smoothie is a treat for both your senses and your soul.

Serving: 2 servings
Preparation Time: 10 minutes
Ready Time: 10 minutes

Ingredients:
- 2 ripe guavas, peeled and diced
- 1 cup frozen pineapple chunks
- 1 banana, peeled and sliced
- 1/2 cup Greek yogurt
- 1 tablespoon honey
- 1/2 cup coconut water
- 1/2 cup ice cubes
- A pinch of salt
- Edible glitter for garnish (optional, for that extra sparkle)

Instructions:
1. In a blender, combine the diced guavas, frozen pineapple chunks, sliced banana, Greek yogurt, honey, coconut water, ice cubes, and a pinch of salt.
2. Blend the ingredients on high speed until smooth and creamy. If the consistency is too thick, you can add more coconut water until you reach your desired thickness.
3. Taste the smoothie and adjust the sweetness by adding more honey if needed.
4. Once the smoothie reaches the desired consistency and taste, pour it into glasses.
5. If you want to add a touch of Billie's signature style, sprinkle some edible glitter on top for that extra flair.
6. Serve the "All The Good Girls Go To Hell Guava Smoothie" immediately and enjoy the rebellious burst of flavors!

Nutrition Information:
(Per serving)
- Calories: 180
- Total Fat: 1g
- Saturated Fat: 0.5g

- Cholesterol: 2mg
- Sodium: 60mg
- Total Carbohydrates: 40g
- Dietary Fiber: 5g
- Sugars: 25g
- Protein: 5g

Note: Nutrition information is approximate and may vary based on specific ingredients used. Adjustments can be made based on dietary preferences and restrictions.

35. Halley's Comet Honeydew Salad

Embark on a celestial culinary journey with the Halley's Comet Honeydew Salad, a dish inspired by the ethereal and otherworldly vibes of Billie Eilish. This refreshing salad combines the sweetness of honeydew melon with a burst of citrus and a touch of mint, creating a flavor experience that's as unique as Billie's musical style.

Serving: 4 servings
Preparation Time: 15 minutes
Ready Time: 30 minutes

Ingredients:
- 1 medium-sized honeydew melon, peeled, seeded, and diced
- 1 cup blueberries
- 1 cup fresh raspberries
- 1 cup cucumber, diced
- 1/4 cup fresh mint leaves, chopped
- Zest and juice of 1 lime
- 2 tablespoons honey
- 1 tablespoon poppy seeds

Instructions:
1. In a large mixing bowl, combine the diced honeydew melon, blueberries, raspberries, and diced cucumber.
2. In a small bowl, whisk together the lime zest, lime juice, and honey. Drizzle this sweet and citrusy dressing over the fruit mixture.
3. Gently toss the salad until the fruit is evenly coated with the dressing.

4. Sprinkle the chopped mint leaves and poppy seeds over the salad, providing a burst of freshness and a delightful crunch.
5. Allow the salad to chill in the refrigerator for at least 15 minutes, allowing the flavors to meld.
6. Before serving, give the salad a final gentle toss to ensure all the ingredients are well combined.
7. Serve the Halley's Comet Honeydew Salad in individual bowls or on a platter, allowing the vibrant colors to shine.

Nutrition Information:
Per serving:
- Calories: 120 kcal
- Total Fat: 0.5g
- Saturated Fat: 0g
- Cholesterol: 0mg
- Sodium: 10mg
- Total Carbohydrates: 30g
- Dietary Fiber: 5g
- Sugars: 20g
- Protein: 2g

Delight in the cosmic fusion of flavors and textures in this Halley's Comet Honeydew Salad—a tribute to Billie Eilish's unique and celestial artistry.

36. I Didn't Change My Number Iceberg Lettuce Wraps

Billie Eilish's bold and unapologetic style is not only reflected in her music but also in her approach to life and, of course, food. These "I Didn't Change My Number Iceberg Lettuce Wraps" pay homage to her hit song while offering a fresh and vibrant twist to your dining experience. Packed with crisp flavors and a touch of rebellious creativity, these lettuce wraps are a celebration of individuality and a perfect addition to any gathering.

Serving: Makes 4 servings.
Preparation Time: 20 minutes.
Ready Time: 20 minutes.

Ingredients:
- 1 lb ground turkey or chicken
- 1 tablespoon olive oil
- 1 onion, finely chopped
- 2 cloves garlic, minced
- 1 teaspoon ground cumin
- 1 teaspoon smoked paprika
- 1 teaspoon chili powder
- Salt and pepper to taste
- 1 cup cherry tomatoes, diced
- 1 cup corn kernels, cooked
- 1 cup black beans, drained and rinsed
- 1/2 cup fresh cilantro, chopped
- 1 head iceberg lettuce, leaves separated

Instructions:
1. In a large skillet, heat olive oil over medium heat. Add chopped onion and garlic, sautéing until softened.
2. Add ground turkey or chicken to the skillet, breaking it apart with a spoon as it cooks. Cook until browned and cooked through.
3. Season the meat with cumin, smoked paprika, chili powder, salt, and pepper. Mix well to incorporate the spices evenly.
4. Stir in diced cherry tomatoes, corn kernels, black beans, and fresh cilantro. Cook for an additional 3-5 minutes until the vegetables are heated through.
5. Carefully separate leaves from the head of iceberg lettuce to create cups for the filling.
6. Spoon the flavorful mixture into each lettuce cup, creating a generous filling in each one.
7. Serve immediately, allowing everyone to enjoy these vibrant and flavorful wraps.

Nutrition Information:
Note: Nutrition information may vary based on specific ingredients used.
- Calories: 320 per serving
- Protein: 25g
- Carbohydrates: 30g
- Dietary Fiber: 8g

- Sugars: 5g
- Fat: 12g
- Saturated Fat: 3g
- Cholesterol: 60mg
- Sodium: 450mg

These "I Didn't Change My Number Iceberg Lettuce Wraps" are not just a feast for the taste buds but also a nod to the eclectic and fearless spirit of Billie Eilish. Enjoy the combination of textures and flavors in each bite, and savor the rebellious energy that inspired this unique dish.

37. My Strange Addiction Mashed Potato Mountains

Embark on a culinary adventure inspired by the unique and eccentric world of Billie Eilish with our creation, "My Strange Addiction Mashed Potato Mountains." This dish pays homage to Billie's bold and unconventional style, offering a whimsical twist on a classic comfort food. Brace yourself for a flavor journey that transcends the ordinary.

Serving: 4 servings
Preparation Time: 20 minutes
Ready Time: 45 minutes

Ingredients:
- 4 large potatoes, peeled and diced
- 1/2 cup butter
- 1/2 cup milk
- Salt and pepper to taste
- 1 cup shredded cheddar cheese
- 1/4 cup chopped chives
- 1/4 cup crispy bacon bits
- 1/4 cup sour cream
- 1/4 cup sliced green onions

Instructions:
1. Boil the diced potatoes in a large pot until fork-tender. Drain and return them to the pot.
2. Mash the potatoes while adding butter, milk, salt, and pepper. Continue mashing until smooth and creamy.

3. In a separate pan, prepare crispy bacon bits.
4. Assemble the Mashed Potato Mountains by shaping the mashed potatoes into four mountain-like peaks on individual serving plates.
5. Sprinkle shredded cheddar cheese generously over each mountain, allowing it to melt slightly.
6. Garnish each mountain with crispy bacon bits, chopped chives, sour cream, and sliced green onions.
7. Serve immediately, allowing your guests to marvel at the edible landscape before indulging in the savory goodness.

Nutrition Information (per serving):
- Calories: 400
- Protein: 10g
- Fat: 20g
- Carbohydrates: 45g
- Fiber: 5g
- Sugar: 2g
- Sodium: 400mg

Dive into the extraordinary flavors of "My Strange Addiction Mashed Potato Mountains" and let your taste buds dance to the beat of Billie Eilish's unique rhythm. This dish is not just a meal; it's a culinary masterpiece that brings together the best of comfort food and avant-garde creativity.

38. Bury A Friend Banana Bread

Inspired by Billie Eilish's hauntingly captivating song "Bury A Friend," this banana bread recipe is a deliciously dark twist on a classic favorite. With rich chocolate undertones and a hint of mystery, it's the perfect treat for those who enjoy a touch of the unconventional. Dive into the unique flavors of the "Bury A Friend Banana Bread" and let your taste buds experience something out of the ordinary.

Serving: Makes one loaf (about 10 slices)
Preparation Time: 15 minutes
Ready Time: 1 hour and 15 minutes (including baking time)

Ingredients:

- 3 ripe bananas, mashed
- 1/2 cup unsalted butter, melted
- 1 teaspoon vanilla extract
- 1 cup granulated sugar
- 1 large egg
- 1 1/2 cups all-purpose flour
- 1/4 cup cocoa powder
- 1 teaspoon baking soda
- 1/2 teaspoon salt
- 1 cup dark chocolate chips

Instructions:
1. Preheat your oven to 350°F (175°C). Grease a 9x5-inch loaf pan and set aside.
2. In a large mixing bowl, mash the ripe bananas with a fork until smooth.
3. Add the melted butter to the mashed bananas and mix well.
4. Stir in the vanilla extract, granulated sugar, and the egg until the mixture is well combined.
5. In a separate bowl, whisk together the flour, cocoa powder, baking soda, and salt.
6. Gradually add the dry ingredients to the wet ingredients, stirring until just combined. Be careful not to overmix.
7. Gently fold in the dark chocolate chips, ensuring they are evenly distributed throughout the batter.
8. Pour the batter into the prepared loaf pan and smooth the top with a spatula.
9. Bake in the preheated oven for 60-70 minutes or until a toothpick inserted into the center comes out clean.
10. Allow the banana bread to cool in the pan for 10 minutes before transferring it to a wire rack to cool completely.

Nutrition Information (per slice, based on 10 slices):
- Calories: 320
- Total Fat: 14g
- Saturated Fat: 8g
- Cholesterol: 40mg
- Sodium: 260mg
- Total Carbohydrates: 47g
- Dietary Fiber: 3g

- Sugars: 28g
- Protein: 4g

Indulge in this unique "Bury A Friend Banana Bread" and let its dark and delightful flavors transport you to a world of culinary intrigue.

39. Bad Guy Butternut Squash Soup

Get ready to immerse your taste buds in the dark and velvety world of "Bad Guy Butternut Squash Soup." Inspired by the hauntingly soulful tunes of Billie Eilish, this soup is as bold and mysterious as her music. With the rich flavors of butternut squash, complemented by a medley of spices, this soup will have you singing its praises long after the last spoonful. Let the culinary adventure begin!

Serving: 4 servings
Preparation Time: 15 minutes
Ready Time: 45 minutes

Ingredients:
- 1 medium-sized butternut squash, peeled, seeded, and diced
- 1 onion, finely chopped
- 2 cloves garlic, minced
- 2 carrots, peeled and diced
- 2 tablespoons olive oil
- 4 cups vegetable broth
- 1 teaspoon ground cumin
- 1/2 teaspoon ground cinnamon
- 1/4 teaspoon ground nutmeg
- Salt and pepper to taste
- 1/2 cup coconut milk
- Fresh parsley for garnish (optional)

Instructions:
1. In a large pot, heat the olive oil over medium heat. Add the chopped onion and garlic, sautéing until they become translucent and aromatic.
2. Add the diced butternut squash and carrots to the pot, stirring occasionally until they start to soften.

3. Pour in the vegetable broth, ensuring the squash and carrots are submerged. Bring the mixture to a gentle boil.
4. Reduce the heat to simmer and add the ground cumin, cinnamon, nutmeg, salt, and pepper. Allow the soup to simmer until the vegetables are tender, approximately 30 minutes.
5. Once the vegetables are soft, use an immersion blender to puree the soup until smooth and creamy. Alternatively, transfer the mixture to a blender in batches, then return it to the pot.
6. Stir in the coconut milk, ensuring it's well incorporated into the soup. Simmer for an additional 5 minutes to meld the flavors.
7. Taste and adjust the seasonings as needed. If you prefer a thinner consistency, add more vegetable broth.
8. Ladle the Bad Guy Butternut Squash Soup into bowls and garnish with fresh parsley if desired.

Nutrition Information:
(Per Serving)
- Calories: 180
- Total Fat: 8g
- Saturated Fat: 3g
- Cholesterol: 0mg
- Sodium: 700mg
- Total Carbohydrates: 28g
- Dietary Fiber: 5g
- Sugars: 6g
- Protein: 3g

Indulge in this musical and flavorful experience that combines the unique vibes of Billie Eilish with the warmth of a comforting bowl of soup. Enjoy the "Bad Guy Butternut Squash Soup" as you delve into the world of creative and inspired cuisine.

40. Copycat Carrot Cake

Indulge your taste buds with a harmonious symphony of flavors inspired by the eclectic and unique style of Billie Eilish. This Copycat Carrot Cake recipe captures the essence of her creativity and brings a sweet melody to your palate. Moist, spiced, and crowned with a velvety cream cheese frosting, this dessert is a celebration of individuality and bold taste. Let the vibrant notes of this Carrot Cake echo the spirit of Billie's music in your kitchen.

Serving: 12 servings
Preparation Time: 20 minutes
Ready Time: 1 hour and 30 minutes

Ingredients:
- 2 cups all-purpose flour
- 1 1/2 teaspoons baking powder
- 1 teaspoon baking soda
- 1/2 teaspoon salt
- 2 teaspoons ground cinnamon
- 1/2 teaspoon ground nutmeg
- 1/2 teaspoon ground ginger
- 1 cup vegetable oil
- 1 cup granulated sugar
- 1 cup brown sugar, packed
- 4 large eggs
- 2 teaspoons vanilla extract
- 2 cups grated carrots
- 1 cup crushed pineapple, drained
- 1/2 cup shredded coconut
- 1/2 cup chopped walnuts or pecans (optional)

Instructions:
1. Preheat your oven to 350°F (175°C). Grease and flour two 9-inch round cake pans.
2. In a medium bowl, whisk together the flour, baking powder, baking soda, salt, cinnamon, nutmeg, and ginger. Set aside.
3. In a large mixing bowl, combine the vegetable oil, granulated sugar, and brown sugar. Beat until well combined.
4. Add the eggs one at a time, beating well after each addition. Stir in the vanilla extract.
5. Gradually add the dry ingredients to the wet ingredients, mixing until just combined.
6. Fold in the grated carrots, crushed pineapple, shredded coconut, and chopped nuts (if using).
7. Divide the batter evenly between the prepared pans and smooth the tops.

8. Bake in the preheated oven for 30-35 minutes or until a toothpick inserted into the center comes out clean.

9. Allow the cakes to cool in the pans for 10 minutes, then transfer them to a wire rack to cool completely.

Cream Cheese Frosting:
- 8 oz cream cheese, softened
- 1/2 cup unsalted butter, softened
- 4 cups powdered sugar
- 1 teaspoon vanilla extract

Cream Cheese Frosting Instructions:
1. In a large bowl, beat the cream cheese and butter until smooth and creamy.
2. Add the powdered sugar gradually, beating well after each addition.
3. Stir in the vanilla extract and beat until the frosting is smooth and fluffy.

Assembling the Cake:
1. Once the cakes are completely cooled, spread a layer of cream cheese frosting on top of one cake layer.
2. Place the second cake layer on top and frost the entire cake with the remaining cream cheese frosting.
3. Optional: Garnish with additional chopped nuts or shredded coconut.

Nutrition Information (per serving):
- Calories: 450
- Total Fat: 24g
- Saturated Fat: 8g
- Trans Fat: 0g
- Cholesterol: 85mg
- Sodium: 320mg
- Total Carbohydrates: 56g
- Dietary Fiber: 2g
- Sugars: 40g
- Protein: 5g

Enjoy your Copycat Carrot Cake inspired by Billie Eilish – a delightful treat for the senses that mirrors the artist's bold and unique style.

41. Ocean Eyes Orange Sorbet

Indulge your taste buds in a melody of refreshing flavors with the "Ocean Eyes Orange Sorbet," inspired by the enchanting world of Billie Eilish. This vibrant and citrusy sorbet pays homage to Billie's soulful music and evokes the essence of her hit song, "Ocean Eyes." Immerse yourself in the sweet serenade of orange as you savor each spoonful of this delightful frozen treat.

Serving: Serves 4
Preparation Time: 15 minutes
Ready Time: 4 hours (including freezing time)

Ingredients:
- 2 cups fresh orange juice (about 4-5 large oranges)
- 1 cup granulated sugar
- 1 tablespoon orange zest
- 1 teaspoon lemon juice
- 1/2 cup water
- Pinch of salt

Instructions:
1. Prepare the Orange Base:
- In a saucepan, combine granulated sugar and water over medium heat. Stir until the sugar dissolves completely.
- Bring the sugar syrup to a gentle boil, then reduce the heat to low and simmer for 5 minutes.
2. Create the Citrus Infusion:
- Add fresh orange juice, orange zest, lemon juice, and a pinch of salt to the sugar syrup.
- Stir the mixture well and let it simmer for an additional 5 minutes to infuse the flavors.
3. Chill the Mixture:
- Remove the saucepan from heat and let the orange mixture cool to room temperature.
- Once cooled, cover the mixture and refrigerate for at least 2 hours to ensure it's thoroughly chilled.
4. Freeze the Sorbet:
- Pour the chilled orange mixture into an ice cream maker and churn according to the manufacturer's instructions.
- Transfer the sorbet into a lidded container and freeze for an additional 2 hours, or until it reaches a scoopable consistency.

5. Serve and Enjoy:
- Scoop the Ocean Eyes Orange Sorbet into bowls or cones.
- Garnish with additional orange zest if desired, and savor the melody of citrus notes reminiscent of Billie Eilish's soulful tunes.

Nutrition Information:
Per Serving (1/2 cup):
- Calories: 120
- Total Fat: 0g
- Cholesterol: 0mg
- Sodium: 10mg
- Total Carbohydrates: 30g
- Dietary Fiber: 0g
- Sugars: 28g
- Protein: 0g

Feel the cool waves of citrusy bliss with every bite of this Ocean Eyes Orange Sorbet – a harmonious fusion of flavor that captures the essence of Billie Eilish's musical artistry.

42. All The Good Girls Go To Hell Artichoke Dip

Indulge your taste buds in a symphony of flavors with the "All The Good Girls Go To Hell Artichoke Dip," a savory creation inspired by the eclectic and bold Billie Eilish. This delectable dip pays homage to the artist's unique style with its rich blend of ingredients that dance together in perfect harmony. Whether you're hosting a gathering or treating yourself to a culinary adventure, this dish is sure to hit all the right notes.

Serving: Ideal for sharing, this recipe yields approximately 8 servings.
Preparation Time: 20 minutes
Ready Time: 35 minutes

Ingredients:
- 1 cup canned artichoke hearts, drained and chopped
- 1 cup mayonnaise
- 1 cup grated Parmesan cheese
- 1 cup shredded mozzarella cheese
- 1/2 cup cream cheese, softened

- 1/4 cup sour cream
- 1/4 cup chopped green onions
- 2 cloves garlic, minced
- 1 teaspoon dried oregano
- 1/2 teaspoon crushed red pepper flakes (adjust to taste)
- Salt and black pepper to taste
- Fresh parsley, chopped (for garnish)

Instructions:
1. Preheat your oven to 375°F (190°C).
2. In a large mixing bowl, combine the chopped artichoke hearts, mayonnaise, grated Parmesan cheese, shredded mozzarella cheese, softened cream cheese, sour cream, chopped green onions, minced garlic, dried oregano, and crushed red pepper flakes. Mix well until all the ingredients are evenly incorporated.
3. Season the mixture with salt and black pepper to taste. Adjust the spice level by adding more crushed red pepper flakes if desired.
4. Transfer the mixture into a baking dish, spreading it evenly.
5. Bake in the preheated oven for approximately 20-25 minutes or until the dip is hot and bubbly, and the top is golden brown.
6. Remove from the oven and let it cool for a few minutes. Garnish with fresh chopped parsley.
7. Serve the "All The Good Girls Go To Hell Artichoke Dip" with your favorite tortilla chips, crackers, or sliced baguette.

Nutrition Information:
Note: Nutritional values are approximate and may vary based on specific ingredients used.
- Calories: 280 per serving
- Total Fat: 25g
- Saturated Fat: 10g
- Trans Fat: 0g
- Cholesterol: 45mg
- Sodium: 450mg
- Total Carbohydrates: 4g
- Dietary Fiber: 1g
- Sugars: 2g
- Protein: 9g

Enjoy this irresistible artichoke dip that captures the essence of Billie Eilish's daring spirit and adds a dash of excitement to your culinary repertoire!

43. Happier Than Ever Honey Ham Sandwich

Get ready to dive into the delectable world of the "Happier Than Ever Honey Ham Sandwich," a culinary creation inspired by the soulful vibes of Billie Eilish. This sandwich is a harmonious blend of sweet and savory, just like the artist's eclectic mix of emotions in her music. Elevate your taste buds with this delightful treat that captures the essence of happiness in every bite.

Serving: Makes 2 sandwiches
Preparation Time: 15 minutes
Ready Time: 20 minutes

Ingredients:
- 1 pound thinly sliced honey ham
- 4 slices Swiss cheese
- 4 slices whole grain bread
- 2 tablespoons Dijon mustard
- 2 tablespoons honey
- 1 medium Granny Smith apple, thinly sliced
- 2 tablespoons mayonnaise
- 1 tablespoon unsalted butter
- Fresh arugula for garnish
- Salt and pepper to taste

Instructions:
1. Prepare the Honey Mustard Spread:
- In a small bowl, mix together Dijon mustard and honey. Set aside.
2. Assemble the Sandwiches:
- Lay out the slices of bread. On two slices, spread a generous layer of the honey mustard mixture.
- On the other two slices, spread a thin layer of mayonnaise.
- On the honey mustard side, layer ham, Swiss cheese, and thinly sliced apples. Sprinkle with salt and pepper to taste.

- Top each with the mayo-spread slices to create two sandwiches.
3. Grill the Sandwiches:
- In a skillet over medium heat, melt butter.
- Place the sandwiches in the skillet and cook for 3-4 minutes on each side or until the bread is golden brown, and the cheese is melted.
4. Serve:
- Remove from the skillet and let them rest for a minute.
- Slice each sandwich diagonally and garnish with fresh arugula.

Nutrition Information:
- (Per serving - 1 sandwich)
- Calories: 550
- Total Fat: 25g
- Saturated Fat: 10g
- Trans Fat: 0g
- Cholesterol: 65mg
- Sodium: 1100mg
- Total Carbohydrates: 56g
- Dietary Fiber: 8g
- Sugars: 20g
- Protein: 28g

Indulge in the symphony of flavors that the Happier Than Ever Honey Ham Sandwich brings to your palate—a true ode to the sensational Billie Eilish.

44. Therefore I Am Tomato Tart

Billie Eilish, the Grammy-winning artist known for her unique style and bold personality, inspires creativity not only in music but also in the culinary world. "Therefore I Am Tomato Tart" is a tribute to her hit song "Therefore I Am," capturing the essence of self-confidence and individuality. This savory tart celebrates the vibrant flavors of fresh tomatoes, bringing together a melody of tastes that will leave your taste buds singing.

Serving: 4-6 servings
Preparation Time: 20 minutes
Ready Time: 45 minutes

Ingredients:
- 1 sheet of puff pastry, thawed
- 1 cup cherry tomatoes, halved
- 2 large tomatoes, sliced
- 1/4 cup sundried tomatoes, chopped
- 1 cup mozzarella cheese, shredded
- 1/4 cup Parmesan cheese, grated
- 2 cloves garlic, minced
- 2 tablespoons olive oil
- 1 tablespoon balsamic glaze
- 1 teaspoon dried oregano
- Salt and pepper to taste
- Fresh basil leaves for garnish

Instructions:
1. Preheat your oven to 400°F (200°C).
2. Roll out the puff pastry on a floured surface and transfer it to a baking sheet lined with parchment paper.
3. In a small bowl, mix the minced garlic with olive oil. Brush the garlic-infused oil over the puff pastry.
4. Layer the mozzarella and Parmesan cheeses evenly over the puff pastry, leaving a border around the edges.
5. Arrange the sliced tomatoes, halved cherry tomatoes, and sundried tomatoes on top of the cheese layer.
6. Drizzle balsamic glaze over the tomatoes and sprinkle with dried oregano. Season with salt and pepper to taste.
7. Fold the edges of the puff pastry over the tomatoes, creating a rustic crust.
8. Bake in the preheated oven for 25-30 minutes or until the pastry is golden and the tomatoes are tender.
9. Remove from the oven and let it cool for a few minutes. Garnish with fresh basil leaves.
10. Slice and serve this delightful "Therefore I Am Tomato Tart" to enjoy a symphony of flavors inspired by Billie Eilish.

Nutrition Information:
(Per serving)
- Calories: 320
- Total Fat: 22g

- Saturated Fat: 7g
- Cholesterol: 20mg
- Sodium: 350mg
- Total Carbohydrates: 22g
- Dietary Fiber: 2g
- Sugars: 3g
- Protein: 10g

Note: Nutrition information is approximate and may vary based on specific ingredients used.

45. NDA Nutella Crepes

Indulge in the sweet symphony of flavors with the NDA Nutella Crepes—a delightful creation inspired by the enigmatic Billie Eilish. Named after her hit single "NDA," these Nutella-infused crepes promise a harmonious blend of rich chocolate hazelnut spread and delicate pancake perfection. Whether you're a fan of Billie's music or simply seeking a delectable treat, these crepes are a celebration of taste that transcends boundaries.

Serving: This recipe yields approximately 8 Nutella Crepes, serving 4 people.
Preparation Time: 15 minutes
Ready Time: 30 minutes

Ingredients:
- 1 cup all-purpose flour
- 2 eggs
- 1/2 cup milk
- 1/2 cup water
- 1/4 teaspoon salt
- 2 tablespoons melted butter
- Nutella (as needed for spreading)
- Fresh strawberries, sliced (for garnish, optional)
- Powdered sugar (for dusting, optional)

Instructions:
1. Prepare the Crepe Batter:

In a blender, combine the flour, eggs, milk, water, salt, and melted butter. Blend until the batter is smooth. Let it rest for 10 minutes.

2. Cook the Crepes:

Heat a non-stick skillet over medium heat. Pour a small amount of batter into the center of the pan, swirling to spread evenly. Cook for about 1-2 minutes, until the edges begin to lift. Flip and cook the other side until golden brown. Repeat with the remaining batter.

3. Spread Nutella:

Once the crepes are cooked, spread a generous layer of Nutella over each crepe. Ensure an even distribution for a decadent experience.

4. Fold and Garnish:

Fold each crepe into quarters or roll them up. Place on a serving plate and garnish with fresh strawberry slices if desired.

5. Dust with Powdered Sugar (Optional):

For an extra touch of sweetness, dust the Nutella Crepes with powdered sugar before serving.

Nutrition Information:

(Per serving, based on 2 crepes)

- Calories: 320
- Total Fat: 16g
- Saturated Fat: 9g
- Cholesterol: 100mg
- Sodium: 280mg
- Total Carbohydrates: 38g
- Dietary Fiber: 2g
- Sugars: 18g
- Protein: 8g

Note: Nutrition information is approximate and may vary based on specific ingredients and serving sizes.

Celebrate the magic of Billie Eilish with every delectable bite of these NDA Nutella Crepes— a symphony of flavors that's both sweet and soulful.

46. Your Power Yellow Zucchini Stir Fry

Fuel your day with vibrant energy and the bold flavors of Billie Eilish-inspired cuisine. Embrace the spirit of innovation and creativity with

"Your Power Yellow Zucchini Stir Fry." This dish captures the essence of Billie's empowering vibes, blending wholesome ingredients into a symphony of taste and color. Get ready to embark on a culinary journey that resonates with the rhythm of Billie Eilish's music.

Serving: 4 servings
Preparation time: 15 minutes
Ready time: 25 minutes

Ingredients:
- 2 yellow zucchinis, thinly sliced
- 1 red bell pepper, thinly sliced
- 1 yellow bell pepper, thinly sliced
- 1 orange bell pepper, thinly sliced
- 1 cup snap peas, trimmed
- 1/4 cup soy sauce
- 2 tablespoons sesame oil
- 1 tablespoon rice vinegar
- 1 tablespoon honey
- 1 tablespoon ginger, minced
- 2 cloves garlic, minced
- 1 teaspoon red pepper flakes (adjust to taste)
- 2 tablespoons vegetable oil
- 2 green onions, sliced (for garnish)
- Sesame seeds (for garnish)
- Cooked rice (optional, for serving)

Instructions:
1. In a small bowl, whisk together soy sauce, sesame oil, rice vinegar, honey, minced ginger, minced garlic, and red pepper flakes. Set aside.
2. Heat vegetable oil in a large wok or skillet over medium-high heat.
3. Add sliced yellow zucchini, red bell pepper, yellow bell pepper, and orange bell pepper to the pan. Stir-fry for 3-4 minutes until the vegetables are slightly tender but still crisp.
4. Add snap peas to the wok and continue to stir-fry for an additional 2 minutes.
5. Pour the prepared sauce over the vegetables and toss everything together to ensure an even coating.
6. Continue to cook for an additional 2-3 minutes, allowing the flavors to meld and the vegetables to absorb the sauce.

7. Once the vegetables are cooked to your liking, remove the stir-fry from heat.
8. Garnish with sliced green onions and sesame seeds for an extra burst of freshness and texture.
9. Serve the "Your Power Yellow Zucchini Stir Fry" over cooked rice if desired.

Nutrition Information (per serving):
- Calories: 180
- Total Fat: 12g
- Saturated Fat: 2g
- Cholesterol: 0mg
- Sodium: 780mg
- Total Carbohydrates: 18g
- Dietary Fiber: 4g
- Sugars: 10g
- Protein: 4g

Immerse yourself in the vibrant colors and flavors of this stir fry, and let it be a celebration of individuality and empowerment inspired by Billie Eilish's music.

47. Not My Responsibility Nectarine Smoothie

Indulge your taste buds in the vibrant world of Billie Eilish-inspired cuisine with the "Not My Responsibility Nectarine Smoothie." Named after one of Billie's iconic tracks, this smoothie is a symphony of flavors that dance together harmoniously. Just like Billie's music, this beverage is an exploration of bold tastes and innovative combinations. Get ready to sip on a blend that's as unique as the artist herself.

Serving: 2 servings
Preparation Time: 10 minutes
Ready Time: 15 minutes

Ingredients:
- 2 ripe nectarines, pitted and sliced
- 1 cup frozen mango chunks
- 1 banana, peeled and sliced

- 1/2 cup Greek yogurt
- 1 tablespoon honey
- 1/2 teaspoon grated fresh ginger
- 1 cup coconut water
- 1/2 cup ice cubes
- Edible flowers for garnish (optional)

Instructions:
1. Prepare the Ingredients: Ensure all the fruits are washed, pitted, and sliced. Measure out the Greek yogurt, honey, grated ginger, and coconut water.
2. Assembly: In a blender, combine the ripe nectarines, frozen mango chunks, sliced banana, Greek yogurt, honey, and grated ginger.
3. Liquid Magic: Pour in the coconut water to add a tropical twist to the mix. If you prefer a thicker consistency, you can reduce the amount of coconut water.
4. Chill Out: Toss in the ice cubes to give your smoothie a refreshing chill. This step is optional if you prefer a room temperature or warmer beverage.
5. Blend Away: Blend all the ingredients until smooth and creamy. Stop and scrape down the sides if needed to ensure an even consistency.
6. Pour and Garnish: Pour the smoothie into glasses and, if you're feeling extra fancy, garnish with edible flowers for a touch of elegance.
7. Serve: Enjoy the "Not My Responsibility Nectarine Smoothie" immediately. Share with a friend or savor it solo while vibing to your favorite Billie Eilish tunes.

Nutrition Information:
Note: Nutrition information is approximate and may vary based on specific ingredients and quantities used.
- Calories per serving: 220
- Total Fat: 2g
- Saturated Fat: 1g
- Cholesterol: 5mg
- Sodium: 50mg
- Total Carbohydrates: 50g
- Dietary Fiber: 6g
- Sugars: 38g
- Protein: 5g

Embark on a sensory journey with this "Not My Responsibility Nectarine Smoothie," a tribute to Billie Eilish's creative spirit and musical genius.

48. Overheated Orange Marmalade

Get ready to experience the vibrant and bold flavors inspired by the one and only Billie Eilish with our "Overheated Orange Marmalade." This zesty and intense spread captures the essence of Billie's dynamic energy, bringing a burst of warmth and citrusy goodness to your taste buds. Perfectly paired with toast, pastries, or as an accompaniment to your favorite dishes, this marmalade is a sensory delight that mirrors Billie's eclectic musical style.

Serving: Yields approximately 2 cups of Overheated Orange Marmalade.
Preparation Time: 15 minutes
Ready Time: 1 hour (including cooling time)

Ingredients:
- 4 large oranges, preferably organic
- 1 lemon, juiced
- 2 cups granulated sugar
- 1/2 cup water
- 1 teaspoon vanilla extract
- Pinch of salt

Instructions:
1. Prepare the Citrus:
- Wash the oranges thoroughly and zest two of them. Set the zest aside.
- Peel all four oranges, removing as much white pith as possible. Section the oranges and remove seeds.
2. Cook the Citrus:
- In a medium saucepan, combine the orange sections, orange zest, lemon juice, and water.
- Bring the mixture to a boil over medium-high heat. Reduce the heat to low and simmer for about 30 minutes, stirring occasionally.
3. Add Sugar and Vanilla:
- Stir in the granulated sugar, vanilla extract, and a pinch of salt.

- Continue to simmer over low heat, stirring occasionally, until the mixture thickens and reaches the desired consistency (approximately 20-30 minutes).
4. Check the Marmalade:
- To test if the marmalade is ready, place a small amount on a chilled plate. If it wrinkles when you push it with your finger, it's ready.
5. Cool and Store:
- Remove the saucepan from the heat and let the marmalade cool for 10 minutes.
- Transfer the marmalade into sterilized jars and let it cool to room temperature before refrigerating.

Nutrition Information:
(Per 1 tablespoon serving)
- Calories: 50
- Total Fat: 0g
- Cholesterol: 0mg
- Sodium: 5mg
- Total Carbohydrates: 13g
- Sugars: 12g
- Protein: 0g
Indulge in the intense flavors of "Overheated Orange Marmalade," a delightful tribute to the artistic brilliance of Billie Eilish. This versatile spread is sure to become a staple in your kitchen, just like Billie's music is a staple in the hearts of fans worldwide.

49. I Love You Lemon Loaf

Indulge your taste buds in the symphony of flavors with the "I Love You Lemon Loaf," a delightful creation inspired by the one and only Billie Eilish. This zesty and tender lemon loaf is a perfect blend of sweet and tart, capturing the essence of Billie's eclectic and dynamic musical style. Whether you're a fan of her music or simply craving a slice of sunshine, this lemon loaf will surely hit all the right notes.

Serving: 8-10 slices
Preparation Time: 15 minutes
Ready Time: 1 hour 15 minutes

Ingredients:
- 1 ½ cups all-purpose flour
- 1 teaspoon baking powder
- ½ teaspoon baking soda
- ½ teaspoon salt
- ½ cup unsalted butter, softened
- 1 cup granulated sugar
- 3 large eggs
- 1 teaspoon vanilla extract
- 2 tablespoons lemon zest
- ¼ cup fresh lemon juice
- ½ cup buttermilk

Instructions:
1. Preheat your oven to 350°F (175°C). Grease and flour a 9x5-inch loaf pan.
2. In a medium bowl, whisk together the flour, baking powder, baking soda, and salt. Set aside.
3. In a large mixing bowl, cream together the softened butter and granulated sugar until light and fluffy.
4. Add the eggs one at a time, beating well after each addition. Stir in the vanilla extract.
5. In a small bowl, combine the lemon zest and lemon juice. Add this mixture to the wet ingredients and mix until well combined.
6. Gradually add the dry ingredients to the wet ingredients, alternating with the buttermilk, beginning and ending with the dry ingredients. Mix until just combined.
7. Pour the batter into the prepared loaf pan, spreading it evenly.
8. Bake in the preheated oven for 55-65 minutes or until a toothpick inserted into the center comes out clean.
9. Allow the lemon loaf to cool in the pan for 15 minutes before transferring it to a wire rack to cool completely.

Nutrition Information:
(Per serving - based on 10 servings)
- Calories: 280
- Total Fat: 12g
- Saturated Fat: 7g
- Cholesterol: 80mg

- Sodium: 260mg
- Total Carbohydrates: 38g
- Dietary Fiber: 1g
- Sugars: 22g
- Protein: 4g

The "I Love You Lemon Loaf" is a sweet testament to the vibrant and eclectic spirit of Billie Eilish's music. Share a slice with loved ones or savor it alone – this lemony delight is bound to make your taste buds sing!

50. Getting Older Grape Gelato

Embrace the soulful notes of Billie Eilish's music with our "Getting Older Grape Gelato." This dessert is a symphony of flavors, blending the richness of grapes with the smooth texture of gelato. It's a sweet tribute to Billie's artistic evolution, just like the progression of flavors in this delightful treat. So, put on your favorite Billie Eilish track and let's dive into creating a dessert as unique and timeless as her music.

Serving: Serves 4
Preparation Time: 15 minutes
Ready Time: 4 hours (including freezing time)

Ingredients:
- 2 cups red seedless grapes, washed and stems removed
- 1 cup sugar
- 2 cups whole milk
- 1 cup heavy cream
- 1 teaspoon vanilla extract
- 1/4 teaspoon salt

Instructions:
1. Prepare the Grapes:
- Place the grapes in a blender or food processor and blend until smooth.
2. Create Grape Syrup:
- In a saucepan over medium heat, combine the grape puree and sugar.
- Stir continuously until the sugar dissolves and the mixture thickens slightly to form a syrup. This usually takes about 5-7 minutes.

- Remove from heat and let it cool.
3. Make the Gelato Base:
- In a separate saucepan, heat the milk and cream over medium heat until it begins to simmer. Do not boil.
- Stir in the vanilla extract and salt.
4. Combine Grape Syrup and Gelato Base:
- Slowly pour the grape syrup into the milk mixture, stirring continuously to combine.
- Let the mixture cool to room temperature.
5. Chill the Mixture:
- Cover the mixture and refrigerate for at least 2 hours or until it's thoroughly chilled.
6. Churn the Gelato:
- Pour the chilled mixture into an ice cream maker and churn according to the manufacturer's instructions.
7. Freeze the Gelato:
- Transfer the churned gelato to a lidded container and freeze for at least 2 hours or until firm.
8. Serve and Enjoy:
- Scoop the Getting Older Grape Gelato into bowls or cones.
- Garnish with fresh grapes or a mint sprig if desired.

Nutrition Information:
Per Serving (1/2 cup):
- Calories: 250
- Total Fat: 15g
- Saturated Fat: 10g
- Trans Fat: 0g
- Cholesterol: 60mg
- Sodium: 90mg
- Total Carbohydrates: 27g
- Dietary Fiber: 1g
- Sugars: 24g
- Protein: 3g

Indulge in the cool, sweet melody of the Getting Older Grape Gelato – a delightful homage to the creativity of Billie Eilish.

51. Lost Cause Lemonade

Embrace the vibrant and rebellious spirit of Billie Eilish with "Lost Cause Lemonade," a refreshing twist on the classic summer beverage. This zesty concoction mirrors the boldness and individuality that defines Billie's music. Sip on this flavorful blend, and let the rebellious notes dance on your taste buds.

Serving: Serves 4
Preparation Time: 15 minutes
Ready Time: 2 hours (including chilling time)

Ingredients:
- 4 cups cold water
- 1 cup freshly squeezed lemon juice (about 6-8 lemons)
- 1/2 cup agave syrup or honey
- 1/2 cup fresh orange juice
- 1 teaspoon grated ginger
- 1/4 teaspoon turmeric powder
- 1/4 teaspoon cayenne pepper (adjust to taste)
- Ice cubes
- Lemon slices and mint leaves for garnish

Instructions:
1. Prepare the Lemonade Base:
- In a pitcher, combine cold water, freshly squeezed lemon juice, agave syrup (or honey), and fresh orange juice. Stir well to ensure the sweeteners dissolve completely.
2. Infuse with Flavor:
- Add grated ginger, turmeric powder, and a hint of cayenne pepper to the lemonade base. These ingredients add a subtle warmth and complexity to the drink. Adjust the cayenne pepper to your preferred level of spiciness.
3. Mix Thoroughly:
- Stir the mixture thoroughly to evenly distribute the flavors. Make sure the ingredients are well incorporated.
4. Chill:
- Place the pitcher in the refrigerator and let the flavors meld for at least 2 hours. This chilling time allows the spices to infuse into the lemonade, creating a harmonious blend.

5. Serve:
- Fill glasses with ice cubes and pour the chilled Lost Cause Lemonade over the ice. Garnish each glass with a slice of lemon and a sprig of fresh mint for an extra burst of flavor and aroma.
6. Enjoy:
- Raise your glass, toast to individuality, and savor the rebellious spirit of this Billie Eilish-inspired beverage.

Nutrition Information:
(Per Serving)
- Calories: 80
- Total Fat: 0g
- Saturated Fat: 0g
- Cholesterol: 0mg
- Sodium: 5mg
- Total Carbohydrates: 21g
- Dietary Fiber: 1g
- Sugars: 16g
- Protein: 1g
Note: Nutrition information is approximate and may vary based on specific ingredients used.

52. Oxytocin Orange Muffins

Indulge your senses in the harmonious blend of flavors with our "Oxytocin Orange Muffins," inspired by the enchanting world of Billie Eilish. Named after the feel-good hormone, these muffins promise a burst of citrusy joy and warmth in every bite. Perfect for a cozy day or whenever you crave a delightful treat, these muffins are sure to become a favorite on your playlist of culinary delights.

Serving: Makes 12 muffins
Preparation Time: 15 minutes
Ready Time: 35 minutes

Ingredients:
- 2 cups all-purpose flour
- 1 cup granulated sugar

- 1 tablespoon baking powder
- 1/2 teaspoon baking soda
- 1/4 teaspoon salt
- 1/2 cup unsalted butter, melted
- 1 cup orange juice (freshly squeezed for best flavor)
- 2 large eggs
- 1 teaspoon vanilla extract
- Zest of one orange
- 1/2 cup plain Greek yogurt

Instructions:
1. Preheat your oven to 375°F (190°C). Line a muffin tin with paper liners.
2. In a large bowl, whisk together the flour, sugar, baking powder, baking soda, and salt.
3. In a separate bowl, combine the melted butter, orange juice, eggs, vanilla extract, orange zest, and Greek yogurt. Mix well until the ingredients are thoroughly combined.
4. Pour the wet ingredients into the dry ingredients and gently fold the mixture until just combined. Be careful not to overmix; a few lumps are okay.
5. Spoon the batter into the prepared muffin cups, filling each about two-thirds full.
6. Bake in the preheated oven for 18-20 minutes or until a toothpick inserted into the center of a muffin comes out clean.
7. Allow the muffins to cool in the tin for 5 minutes, then transfer them to a wire rack to cool completely.

Nutrition Information:
Per Serving (1 muffin)
- Calories: 220
- Total Fat: 8g
- Saturated Fat: 5g
- Cholesterol: 45mg
- Sodium: 200mg
- Total Carbohydrates: 33g
- Dietary Fiber: 1g
- Sugars: 16g
- Protein: 4g

Elevate your baking experience with these Oxytocin Orange Muffins, a symphony of citrusy notes that echo the vibrant spirit of Billie Eilish. Enjoy the warm embrace of these muffins as they fill your kitchen with the sweet aroma of joy and connection.

53. My Future Fig Salad

Billie Eilish, with her unique style and bold creativity, has inspired not only the music world but also the culinary realm. "My Future Fig Salad" is a delightful and refreshing dish that captures the essence of Billie's eclectic taste. With the sweet allure of fresh figs and a medley of vibrant ingredients, this salad is a harmonious blend of flavors that promises to transport you to a world of culinary innovation.

Serving: 4 servings
Preparation Time: 15 minutes
Ready Time: 20 minutes

Ingredients:
- 8 fresh figs, quartered
- 2 cups arugula, washed and dried
- 1 cup cherry tomatoes, halved
- 1/2 cup crumbled feta cheese
- 1/4 cup chopped fresh mint
- 1/4 cup chopped toasted walnuts
- 1/4 cup extra-virgin olive oil
- 2 tablespoons balsamic vinegar
- 1 tablespoon honey
- Salt and pepper to taste

Instructions:
1. Prepare the Dressing:
- In a small bowl, whisk together the extra-virgin olive oil, balsamic vinegar, honey, salt, and pepper. Set aside.
2. Assemble the Salad:
- In a large salad bowl, combine the arugula, quartered figs, halved cherry tomatoes, crumbled feta cheese, chopped fresh mint, and toasted walnuts.

3. Drizzle with Dressing:
- Pour the prepared dressing over the salad ingredients.
4. Toss Gently:
- Toss the salad gently, ensuring that the dressing evenly coats all the ingredients.
5. Serve:
- Divide the salad among four plates.
6. Garnish:
- Garnish with extra mint leaves and a sprinkle of crumbled feta on top.
7. Enjoy:
- Serve immediately and savor the vibrant flavors of "My Future Fig Salad."

Nutrition Information:
- *Per Serving:*
- Calories: 280
- Total Fat: 18g
- Saturated Fat: 4g
- Cholesterol: 15mg
- Sodium: 220mg
- Total Carbohydrates: 28g
- Dietary Fiber: 5g
- Sugars: 20g
- Protein: 6g

Embrace the future with this Billie Eilish-inspired salad, a culinary journey that mirrors the artist's fearless approach to creativity. "My Future Fig Salad" is not just a dish; it's a sensory experience that invites you to savor the present and anticipate the delicious possibilities that lie ahead.

54. Goldwing Ginger Snap Cookies

In the vibrant tapestry of Billie Eilish's creativity, inspiration is woven into every note and lyric. Her music often reflects a blend of boldness and finesse, much like these Goldwing Ginger Snap Cookies. Harnessing the fiery essence of Billie's spirit, these cookies offer a zesty kick and a sweet warmth that's sure to resonate with fans and food enthusiasts alike.

Serving: Makes about 24 cookies
Preparation time: 15 minutes
Ready time: 30 minutes

Ingredients:
- 2 cups all-purpose flour
- 1 teaspoon baking soda
- 1 tablespoon ground ginger
- 1 teaspoon ground cinnamon
- 1/2 teaspoon ground cloves
- 1/4 teaspoon salt
- 3/4 cup unsalted butter, softened
- 1 cup granulated sugar, plus extra for rolling
- 1 large egg
- 1/4 cup molasses

Instructions:
1. Preheat your oven to 350°F (175°C). Line baking sheets with parchment paper.
2. In a medium bowl, whisk together the flour, baking soda, ginger, cinnamon, cloves, and salt until well combined. Set aside.
3. In a large mixing bowl, beat the softened butter and 1 cup of sugar together until light and fluffy.
4. Add the egg and molasses to the butter-sugar mixture. Beat until well incorporated.
5. Gradually add the dry ingredients to the wet mixture, mixing until a smooth dough forms.
6. Take tablespoon-sized portions of dough and roll them into balls. Roll each ball in granulated sugar to coat evenly.
7. Place the sugar-coated dough balls onto the prepared baking sheets, leaving space between each cookie for spreading.
8. Bake for 10-12 minutes or until the edges are firm and the centers are slightly soft.
9. Remove from the oven and let the cookies cool on the baking sheets for 5 minutes before transferring them to a wire rack to cool completely.

Nutrition Information (per serving - 1 cookie):
- Calories: 130
- Total Fat: 6g
- Saturated Fat: 4g

- Trans Fat: 0g
- Cholesterol: 25mg
- Sodium: 85mg
- Total Carbohydrates: 19g
- Dietary Fiber: 0.5g
- Sugars: 10g
- Protein: 1.5g

Enjoy these Goldwing Ginger Snap Cookies, where the spice of ginger meets the sweetness of molasses—a taste that mirrors the electric fusion found in Billie Eilish's music.

55. Your Power Yellow Curry

Indulge in the vibrant and electrifying flavors of "Your Power Yellow Curry," a culinary creation inspired by the sensational Billie Eilish. This dish reflects the boldness and creativity that defines Billie's music, offering a symphony of aromatic spices and wholesome ingredients that come together in a harmonious fusion. Let this curry be a manifestation of your culinary power and a celebration of individuality.

Serving: 4 servings
Preparation Time: 15 minutes
Ready Time: 45 minutes

Ingredients:
- 1 lb (450g) boneless, skinless chicken thighs, cut into bite-sized pieces
- 2 tablespoons yellow curry paste
- 1 can (14 oz/400ml) coconut milk
- 1 large potato, peeled and diced
- 1 large carrot, sliced
- 1 bell pepper, thinly sliced
- 1 onion, finely chopped
- 2 cloves garlic, minced
- 1 tablespoon ginger, grated
- 2 tablespoons vegetable oil
- 1 tablespoon fish sauce (optional for non-vegetarian version)
- 1 tablespoon soy sauce
- 1 tablespoon brown sugar

- 1 lime, juiced
- Fresh cilantro, for garnish
- Cooked jasmine rice, for serving

Instructions:
1. In a large pot or deep skillet, heat vegetable oil over medium heat. Add chopped onion, minced garlic, and grated ginger. Sauté until the onion becomes translucent.
2. Add yellow curry paste to the pot and stir well, allowing the spices to release their flavors. Cook for 2-3 minutes until fragrant.
3. Add chicken pieces to the pot and cook until they are browned on all sides.
4. Pour in the coconut milk, stirring to combine with the curry paste and chicken. Bring the mixture to a gentle simmer.
5. Add diced potatoes, sliced carrots, and bell pepper to the pot. If you're preparing the non-vegetarian version, add fish sauce at this stage for an extra depth of flavor.
6. Season the curry with soy sauce, brown sugar, and lime juice. Stir well and let the curry simmer for 25-30 minutes or until the vegetables are tender and the chicken is fully cooked.
7. Adjust seasoning to taste. If you prefer a spicier curry, you can add more curry paste.
8. Serve the yellow curry over a bed of jasmine rice. Garnish with fresh cilantro for a burst of color and added freshness.

Nutrition Information (per serving):
Note: Nutrition information may vary based on specific ingredients and quantities used.
- Calories: 450
- Protein: 25g
- Fat: 30g
- Carbohydrates: 20g
- Fiber: 3g
- Sugar: 6g
- Sodium: 800mg

Dive into the bold flavors of "Your Power Yellow Curry" and savor the unique blend of ingredients that pay homage to the creativity of Billie Eilish. This dish is a testament to the power of individual expression and culinary exploration.

56. NDA Nectarine Tart

Inspired by the vibrant and eclectic spirit of Billie Eilish, the NDA Nectarine Tart captures the essence of her creativity and uniqueness. This delectable dessert harmonizes the sweetness of ripe nectarines with a delicate crust, inviting you to savor every bite with the same anticipation as awaiting a new Billie Eilish track.

Serving: 8 servings
Preparation time: 25 minutes
Ready time: 1 hour 30 minutes

Ingredients:
For the crust:
- 1 1/4 cups all-purpose flour
- 1/4 cup granulated sugar
- 1/2 cup unsalted butter, chilled and cubed
- 1 egg yolk
- 2 tablespoons ice water
For the filling:
- 4-5 ripe nectarines, thinly sliced
- 1/4 cup apricot preserves
- 2 tablespoons honey
- 1 tablespoon lemon juice
- 1 teaspoon vanilla extract
- 2 tablespoons cornstarch

Instructions:
1. Preheat your oven to 375°F (190°C).
2. For the crust, in a food processor, combine the flour and sugar. Add the chilled butter and pulse until the mixture resembles coarse crumbs.
3. Add the egg yolk and ice water, pulsing until the dough comes together. Form the dough into a disk, wrap it in plastic wrap, and refrigerate for 30 minutes.
4. Roll out the chilled dough on a floured surface to fit a 9-inch tart pan. Carefully place the dough into the pan, pressing it gently into the corners. Trim any excess dough from the edges.

5. In a small bowl, mix the apricot preserves, honey, lemon juice, vanilla extract, and cornstarch until well combined.
6. Arrange the sliced nectarines in overlapping circles on the prepared crust. Brush the nectarines with the apricot glaze mixture.
7. Bake the tart in the preheated oven for 40-45 minutes or until the crust is golden brown, and the nectarines are tender.
8. Once baked, allow the tart to cool on a wire rack for at least 30 minutes before serving.

Nutrition Information (per serving):
- Calories: 280
- Total Fat: 13g
- Saturated Fat: 8g
- Cholesterol: 55mg
- Sodium: 5mg
- Total Carbohydrate: 39g
- Dietary Fiber: 2g
- Sugars: 20g
- Protein: 3g

Enjoy the NDA Nectarine Tart as a delightful homage to Billie Eilish's unique artistry – a sweet symphony of flavors bound to captivate your taste buds.

57. Therefore I Am Tofu Tacos

Indulge in the rebellious spirit of Billie Eilish with these "Therefore I Am Tofu Tacos." This recipe captures the essence of self-expression and bold flavors, mirroring Billie's unapologetic approach to life and music. Packed with vibrant ingredients and savory sensations, these tacos are a celebration of individuality that will leave your taste buds dancing to their own beat.

Serving: 4 servings
Preparation Time: 20 minutes
Ready Time: 35 minutes

Ingredients:
- 1 block (14 oz) extra-firm tofu, pressed and crumbled

- 2 tablespoons soy sauce
- 1 tablespoon olive oil
- 1 teaspoon chili powder
- 1 teaspoon cumin
- 1/2 teaspoon smoked paprika
- 1/2 teaspoon garlic powder
- 1/4 teaspoon black pepper
- 8 small corn tortillas
- 1 cup shredded purple cabbage
- 1 avocado, sliced
- 1/2 cup diced tomatoes
- 1/4 cup chopped red onion
- Fresh cilantro, for garnish
- Lime wedges, for serving

Instructions:
1. Prepare the Tofu:
- Press the tofu to remove excess water, then crumble it into a bowl.
- In a small bowl, whisk together soy sauce, olive oil, chili powder, cumin, smoked paprika, garlic powder, and black pepper.
- Pour the marinade over the crumbled tofu, ensuring it's well-coated. Let it marinate for at least 15 minutes.
2. Cook the Tofu:
- Heat a skillet over medium heat. Add the marinated tofu and cook until it's golden brown and slightly crispy, about 10-12 minutes. Stir occasionally to ensure even cooking.
3. Warm the Tortillas:
- In a dry skillet, warm the corn tortillas for about 20 seconds on each side or until pliable.
4. Assemble the Tacos:
- Spoon the seasoned tofu onto each tortilla.
- Top with shredded purple cabbage, sliced avocado, diced tomatoes, and chopped red onion.
- Garnish with fresh cilantro and serve with lime wedges on the side.
5. Serve and Enjoy:
- Serve the "Therefore I Am Tofu Tacos" immediately, inviting everyone to customize their tacos with additional toppings like hot sauce or salsa.

Nutrition Information (per serving):
- Calories: 280

- Protein: 12g
- Fat: 15g
- Carbohydrates: 28g
- Fiber: 7g
- Sugar: 2g
- Sodium: 480mg

Embrace the rebellious flavors of these tacos and savor each bite with the fearless spirit that echoes Billie Eilish's unique style.

58. Overheated Orange Julius

Indulge in the electrifying flavors of the "Overheated Orange Julius," a beverage that captures the essence of Billie Eilish's bold and vibrant style. This concoction pays homage to the artist's fiery personality, blending the classic Orange Julius with a touch of heat for a unique twist. Get ready to savor the unexpected and enjoy this energizing beverage that mirrors the intensity of Billie's music.

Serving: 2 servings
Preparation Time: 10 minutes
Ready Time: 15 minutes

Ingredients:
- 2 cups fresh orange juice
- 1 cup ice cubes
- 1/2 cup vanilla ice cream
- 2 tablespoons honey
- 1/4 teaspoon cayenne pepper
- Orange slices for garnish (optional)

Instructions:
1. In a blender, combine fresh orange juice, ice cubes, vanilla ice cream, and honey.
2. Blend the mixture on high speed until smooth and creamy.
3. Gradually add cayenne pepper to the blend, adjusting to taste for the desired level of heat.
4. Continue blending until the cayenne pepper is evenly incorporated into the mixture.

5. Pour the Overheated Orange Julius into glasses.

6. Garnish with orange slices if desired.

7. Serve immediately and enjoy the fusion of sweet, creamy, and spicy flavors.

Nutrition Information:

Note: Nutrition values are approximate and may vary based on specific ingredients used.

- Calories: 180 per serving
- Total Fat: 3g
- Saturated Fat: 2g
- Trans Fat: 0g
- Cholesterol: 15mg
- Sodium: 30mg
- Total Carbohydrates: 38g
- Dietary Fiber: 1g
- Sugars: 32g
- Protein: 2g
- Vitamin D: 2%
- Calcium: 6%
- Iron: 2%
- Potassium: 480mg

Elevate your taste buds with the Overheated Orange Julius, a delightful creation inspired by the bold and unique style of Billie Eilish. This drink is sure to become a favorite for those who crave a burst of flavor and a hint of heat in every sip.

59. All The Good Girls Go To Hell Apple Tart

Indulge in the rebellious flavors of Billie Eilish with our "All The Good Girls Go To Hell Apple Tart." This delectable dessert is inspired by the edgy and bold spirit of Billie's music. It's a tantalizing treat that combines the sweetness of apples with a touch of darkness, making it a perfect addition to our collection of 98 Food Ideas Inspired by Billie Eilish. Get ready to experience a burst of flavors that will leave your taste buds singing!

Serving: Serves 8

Preparation Time: 20 minutes
Ready Time: 1 hour and 30 minutes (including baking time)

Ingredients:
- 6 medium-sized apples, peeled, cored, and thinly sliced
- 1 tablespoon lemon juice
- 1/2 cup granulated sugar
- 1 teaspoon ground cinnamon
- 1/4 teaspoon ground nutmeg
- 1 package (17.3 ounces) puff pastry sheets, thawed
- 2 tablespoons unsalted butter, melted
- 2 tablespoons apricot preserves
- Powdered sugar for dusting (optional)

Instructions:
1. Preheat the Oven:
Preheat your oven to 375°F (190°C).
2. Prepare the Apples:
In a large bowl, toss the thinly sliced apples with lemon juice to prevent browning. Add granulated sugar, cinnamon, and nutmeg, tossing until the apples are evenly coated. Set aside and let them macerate for about 10 minutes.
3. Roll Out the Puff Pastry:
Roll out the puff pastry sheets on a floured surface to fit your tart pan. Place the pastry in the pan, pressing it gently against the sides.
4. Arrange the Apple Slices:
Starting from the edges, arrange the apple slices in a circular pattern, slightly overlapping each other. Continue until the entire pastry is covered with the apple slices.
5. Brush with Butter:
Brush the melted butter over the arranged apples to add a golden touch.
6. Bake:
Place the tart in the preheated oven and bake for 40-45 minutes or until the pastry is golden and the apples are tender.
7. Apricot Glaze:
In a small saucepan, heat the apricot preserves over low heat until melted. Brush the melted preserves over the warm tart to add a glossy finish.
8. Cool and Serve:

Allow the tart to cool slightly before slicing. Optionally, dust with powdered sugar for an extra touch of sweetness.

Nutrition Information:
(Per Serving)
- Calories: 280
- Fat: 14g
- Saturated Fat: 4g
- Cholesterol: 10mg
- Sodium: 120mg
- Carbohydrates: 36g
- Fiber: 3g
- Sugars: 18g
- Protein: 2g

Now, revel in the sinfully delicious "All The Good Girls Go To Hell Apple Tart" inspired by the one and only Billie Eilish!

60. Your Power Yellowtail Sashimi

Get ready to experience the bold and vibrant flavors inspired by the incomparable Billie Eilish with "Your Power Yellowtail Sashimi." This dish reflects the artist's fearless approach to creativity, blending contrasting elements to create a symphony of tastes that dance on your palate. The succulent yellowtail sashimi, paired with zesty citrus and a hint of spice, is a culinary masterpiece that echoes Billie's eclectic and daring style.

Serving: Serves 4
Preparation Time: 15 minutes
Ready Time: 20 minutes

Ingredients:
- 1 lb fresh yellowtail fillet, sashimi-grade
- 1 tablespoon soy sauce
- 1 tablespoon ponzu sauce
- 1 teaspoon sesame oil
- 1 teaspoon sriracha sauce (adjust to taste for desired spice level)
- 1 teaspoon honey

- 1 teaspoon fresh ginger, finely grated
- 1 teaspoon lime zest
- 1 tablespoon fresh lime juice
- 1 tablespoon fresh orange juice
- 1 tablespoon green onions, finely sliced (for garnish)
- 1 tablespoon cilantro leaves, chopped (for garnish)
- Sesame seeds for garnish
- Thinly sliced radishes for garnish (optional)

Instructions:
1. Begin by placing the yellowtail fillet in the freezer for about 15 minutes. This will make it easier to slice thinly.
2. While the fish is chilling, prepare the sauce by whisking together soy sauce, ponzu sauce, sesame oil, sriracha, honey, grated ginger, lime zest, lime juice, and orange juice in a bowl. Set aside.
3. Remove the yellowtail from the freezer and slice it thinly against the grain.
4. Arrange the yellowtail slices on a serving platter.
5. Drizzle the prepared sauce over the yellowtail slices, ensuring each piece is well coated.
6. Garnish with sliced green onions, cilantro, sesame seeds, and optional radish slices.
7. Allow the dish to marinate for about 5 minutes to let the flavors meld.
8. Serve immediately and enjoy the vibrant fusion of flavors in "Your Power Yellowtail Sashimi."

Nutrition Information:
(Per serving)
- Calories: 180
- Protein: 22g
- Fat: 8g
- Carbohydrates: 5g
- Fiber: 1g
- Sugar: 3g
- Sodium: 600mg
Note: Nutrition information is approximate and may vary based on specific ingredients used. Adjust quantities and ingredients based on personal dietary preferences and restrictions.

61. Getting Older Grilled Cheese Sandwich

Celebrate the essence of growing older with the "Getting Older Grilled Cheese Sandwich," a comforting and nostalgic dish inspired by the introspective and soulful vibes of Billie Eilish. This sandwich captures the essence of time passing and the beauty found in simplicity, much like the evolution of a classic grilled cheese.

Serving: Makes 2 sandwiches
Preparation Time: 15 minutes
Ready Time: 20 minutes

Ingredients:
- 4 slices of your favorite bread (sourdough recommended)
- 1 cup shredded sharp cheddar cheese
- 1 cup shredded Gruyère cheese
- 1/4 cup unsalted butter, softened
- 1 tablespoon Dijon mustard
- 1 teaspoon garlic powder
- Salt and pepper to taste

Instructions:
1. Preheat the Grill:
- Preheat a skillet or griddle over medium heat.
2. Butter the Bread:
- Spread a generous layer of softened butter on one side of each bread slice.
3. Build the Sandwich:
- On the unbuttered side of two bread slices, spread a thin layer of Dijon mustard.
- In a bowl, mix the shredded cheddar and Gruyère cheeses together. Divide the cheese mixture evenly over the Dijon-covered slices.
- Sprinkle a pinch of garlic powder on top of the cheese on each slice.
- Place the remaining slices of bread, buttered side up, on top to form sandwiches.
4. Grill the Sandwiches:
- Place the sandwiches on the preheated skillet or griddle. Cook until the bread turns golden brown, and the cheese starts to melt, approximately 3-4 minutes per side.
5. Serve:

- Remove the sandwiches from the heat and let them rest for a minute. Slice diagonally and serve warm.

6. Enjoy:
- Embrace the simplicity and deliciousness of the "Getting Older Grilled Cheese Sandwich." Pair it with your favorite dipping sauce or enjoy it on its own.

Nutrition Information:
(Per Serving)
- Calories: 540 kcal
- Total Fat: 38g
- Saturated Fat: 24g
- Trans Fat: 0g
- Cholesterol: 110mg
- Sodium: 700mg
- Total Carbohydrates: 26g
- Dietary Fiber: 2g
- Sugars: 2g
- Protein: 24g

Indulge in this flavorful and melty tribute to Billie Eilish's journey through time, where each bite is a celebration of the past, present, and the simple joys found in the music of life.

62. My Strange Addiction Mushroom Pizza

Indulge your taste buds in the eccentric symphony of flavors with the "My Strange Addiction Mushroom Pizza," inspired by the unique and avant-garde style of the one and only Billie Eilish. This unconventional pizza is a delightful fusion of earthy mushrooms, bold spices, and a hint of rebellious creativity. Embark on a culinary journey that mirrors Billie's genre-defying music, pushing boundaries and challenging the ordinary. Get ready to savor every bite of this extraordinary pizza that captures the essence of Billie Eilish's unconventional spirit.

Serving: Makes 2 medium-sized pizzas
Preparation Time: 15 minutes
Ready Time: 25 minutes

Ingredients:
- 2 pizza dough balls (store-bought or homemade)
- 1 cup tomato sauce
- 2 cups shredded mozzarella cheese
- 1 cup assorted mushrooms, sliced (shiitake, cremini, oyster, or your preference)
- 1/2 red onion, thinly sliced
- 2 cloves garlic, minced
- 1 teaspoon olive oil
- 1 teaspoon dried oregano
- 1/2 teaspoon red pepper flakes (adjust to taste)
- Salt and black pepper to taste
- Fresh basil leaves for garnish

Instructions:
1. Preheat your oven to 450°F (230°C).
2. Roll out the pizza dough on a floured surface to your desired thickness.
3. Place the rolled-out dough on a pizza stone or baking sheet.
4. In a small pan, sauté the sliced mushrooms, red onion, and minced garlic in olive oil until they are tender. Season with salt and black pepper.
5. Spread a thin layer of tomato sauce over the pizza dough, leaving a small border around the edges.
6. Sprinkle a generous amount of shredded mozzarella cheese over the sauce.
7. Distribute the sautéed mushroom mixture evenly over the cheese.
8. Sprinkle dried oregano and red pepper flakes over the top for an extra kick.
9. Bake in the preheated oven for 15-20 minutes or until the crust is golden and the cheese is bubbly.
10. Remove from the oven and let it cool for a few minutes before slicing.
11. Garnish with fresh basil leaves before serving.

Nutrition Information:
(Per serving, based on 8 slices)
- Calories: 280
- Total Fat: 10g
- Saturated Fat: 5g
- Cholesterol: 25mg

- Sodium: 500mg
- Total Carbohydrates: 35g
- Dietary Fiber: 2g
- Sugars: 3g
- Protein: 12g

Indulge in the "My Strange Addiction Mushroom Pizza" for a taste experience that mirrors Billie Eilish's eclectic style and celebrates the unconventional in every bite.

63. Goldwing Garlic Knots

Elevate your taste buds with the enchanting flavors of the "Goldwing Garlic Knots," inspired by the unique style and creativity of Billie Eilish. These golden knots of perfection are not just a treat for the palate but a tribute to the bold and extraordinary. Get ready to indulge in a symphony of garlic-infused goodness that will leave you singing with joy.

Serving: Makes approximately 12 garlic knots.
Preparation Time: 15 minutes
Ready Time: 1 hour 30 minutes (including rising time)

Ingredients:
- 1 pound (about 4 cups) all-purpose flour
- 1 tablespoon sugar
- 2 1/4 teaspoons (1 packet) active dry yeast
- 1 1/2 teaspoons salt
- 1 cup warm water (110°F/43°C)
- 2 tablespoons olive oil
For the Garlic Butter:
- 1/2 cup unsalted butter, melted
- 4 cloves garlic, minced
- 2 tablespoons fresh parsley, finely chopped
- Salt to taste

Instructions:
1. Activate the Yeast:
In a small bowl, combine warm water and sugar. Sprinkle the yeast over the water and let it sit for 5-10 minutes until it becomes frothy.

2. Prepare the Dough:

In a large mixing bowl, combine the flour and salt. Make a well in the center and pour in the activated yeast mixture and olive oil. Mix until a dough forms. Knead the dough on a floured surface for about 5-7 minutes until it becomes smooth and elastic.

3. First Rise:

Place the dough in a greased bowl, cover it with a damp cloth, and let it rise in a warm place for 1 hour or until it has doubled in size.

4. Forming the Knots:

Preheat the oven to 375°F (190°C). Punch down the risen dough and divide it into 12 equal portions. Roll each portion into a long rope and tie it into a knot. Place the knots on a baking sheet lined with parchment paper.

5. Second Rise:

Cover the knots with a damp cloth and let them rise for an additional 30 minutes.

6. Bake:

Bake the knots in the preheated oven for 15-20 minutes or until they are golden brown.

7. Prepare Garlic Butter:

While the knots are baking, mix the melted butter, minced garlic, chopped parsley, and salt in a bowl.

8. Garlic Infusion:

Once the knots are out of the oven, brush them generously with the garlic butter mixture.

9. Serve:

Allow the knots to cool slightly before serving. Enjoy the Goldwing Garlic Knots on their own or as a delightful accompaniment to your favorite dishes.

Nutrition Information:

(Per serving, based on 12 servings)

- Calories: 250
- Total Fat: 10g
- Saturated Fat: 5g
- Trans Fat: 0g
- Cholesterol: 20mg
- Sodium: 300mg
- Total Carbohydrates: 35g
- Dietary Fiber: 2g

- Sugars: 1g
- Protein: 5g
Note: Nutrition information is approximate and may vary based on specific ingredients and portion sizes.

64. Therefore I Am Tomato Basil Bruschetta

Embrace the vibrant flavors of Billie Eilish's eclectic world with the "Therefore I Am Tomato Basil Bruschetta." This delectable bruschetta captures the essence of Billie's bold and unapologetic style, combining fresh ingredients to create a symphony of taste that's as unique as the artist herself.

Serving: Ideal for 4 servings.
Preparation Time: 15 minutes
Ready Time: 20 minutes

Ingredients:
- 1 baguette, sliced
- 4 large tomatoes, diced
- 1/2 cup fresh basil, chopped
- 2 cloves garlic, minced
- 1/4 cup red onion, finely chopped
- 3 tablespoons extra-virgin olive oil
- 1 tablespoon balsamic vinegar
- Salt and pepper to taste
- 1/2 cup crumbled feta cheese (optional, for garnish)

Instructions:
1. Preheat the Oven:
Preheat your oven to 375°F (190°C).
2. Toast the Baguette Slices:
Arrange the baguette slices on a baking sheet and toast them in the preheated oven until they are golden brown and crisp. This usually takes about 5-7 minutes. Keep an eye on them to prevent burning.
3. Prepare the Tomato Basil Mixture:
In a large bowl, combine the diced tomatoes, chopped basil, minced garlic, finely chopped red onion, extra-virgin olive oil, balsamic vinegar,

salt, and pepper. Gently toss the mixture until all the ingredients are well combined.

4. Let the Flavors Mingle:

Allow the tomato basil mixture to sit for about 5 minutes. This gives the flavors time to meld together, creating a more harmonious taste.

5. Top the Toasted Baguette:

Spoon the tomato basil mixture generously over the toasted baguette slices. Ensure an even distribution of the mixture on each slice.

6. Optional Garnish:

For an extra burst of flavor, sprinkle crumbled feta cheese over the bruschetta.

7. Serve and Enjoy:

Arrange the bruschetta on a serving platter and delight in the vibrant flavors of the "Therefore I Am Tomato Basil Bruschetta."

Nutrition Information:

(Per serving)
- Calories: 220
- Total Fat: 10g
- Saturated Fat: 2g
- Trans Fat: 0g
- Cholesterol: 5mg
- Sodium: 350mg
- Total Carbohydrates: 28g
- Dietary Fiber: 2g
- Sugars: 3g
- Protein: 6g

Note: Nutrition information is approximate and may vary based on specific ingredients and serving sizes.

65. Halley's Comet Honey Glazed Carrots

Inspired by the cosmic and vibrant energy of Billie Eilish, these Halley's Comet Honey Glazed Carrots are a sweet symphony of flavors that will transport your taste buds to another dimension. Just like a comet streaking across the sky, these carrots are glazed to perfection, creating a dish that's as visually stunning as it is delicious. Billie's eclectic style and bold personality serve as the muse for this delightful recipe that will add a burst of color and flavor to your table.

Serving: 4 servings
Preparation Time: 15 minutes
Ready Time: 30 minutes

Ingredients:
- 1 pound (about 450g) baby carrots, washed and peeled
- 2 tablespoons olive oil
- 2 tablespoons honey
- 1 tablespoon balsamic vinegar
- 1 teaspoon Dijon mustard
- 1/2 teaspoon garlic powder
- Salt and pepper, to taste
- Fresh parsley, chopped (for garnish)

Instructions:
1. Preheat your oven to 400°F (200°C).
2. In a bowl, whisk together the olive oil, honey, balsamic vinegar, Dijon mustard, and garlic powder. Season with salt and pepper to taste.
3. Place the baby carrots on a baking sheet, and drizzle the honey glaze over them. Toss the carrots to ensure they are evenly coated.
4. Roast the carrots in the preheated oven for about 25-30 minutes or until they are tender, stirring halfway through to ensure even cooking.
5. Once the carrots are caramelized and fork-tender, remove them from the oven.
6. Transfer the glazed carrots to a serving dish, and sprinkle chopped fresh parsley over the top for a burst of color and freshness.
7. Serve the Halley's Comet Honey Glazed Carrots as a delightful side dish that complements a variety of main courses.

Nutrition Information:
Note: Nutritional values are approximate and may vary based on specific ingredients and serving sizes.
- Calories: 150 per serving
- Total Fat: 7g
- Saturated Fat: 1g
- Trans Fat: 0g
- Cholesterol: 0mg

- Sodium: 120mg
- Total Carbohydrates: 23g
- Dietary Fiber: 3g
- Sugars: 15g
- Protein: 1g

Enjoy the celestial flavors of these Halley's Comet Honey Glazed Carrots – a perfect embodiment of Billie Eilish's eclectic spirit on your plate!

66. I Love You Iced Tea

Billie Eilish, the trailblazing artist with a penchant for bold and unique expressions, has inspired not just the music scene but also a generation's approach to individuality. In celebration of her creativity, we present the "I Love You Iced Tea" — a refreshing beverage that mirrors the eclectic spirit of Billie herself. This iced tea is a harmonious blend of flavors that will soothe your senses and make your taste buds sing in harmony.

Serving: This recipe serves 4.
Preparation Time: 15 minutes
Ready Time: 2 hours (including chilling time)

Ingredients:
- 4 cups water
- 4 black tea bags
- 1/2 cup honey
- 1/4 cup fresh lemon juice
- 1/4 cup fresh orange juice
- 1 teaspoon lavender buds (dried)
- 1/2 teaspoon vanilla extract
- Ice cubes
- Lemon and orange slices for garnish

Instructions:
1. Boil the Water:
In a medium-sized pot, bring 4 cups of water to a boil.
2. Steep the Tea:

Add the black tea bags to the boiling water and let them steep for 5-7 minutes. Remove the tea bags and allow the tea to cool to room temperature.

3. Sweeten with Honey:

Once the tea has cooled, stir in the honey until fully dissolved.

4. Infuse with Flavors:

Add the fresh lemon juice, fresh orange juice, lavender buds, and vanilla extract to the tea. Stir well to combine.

5. Chill the Tea:

Place the tea in the refrigerator and let it chill for at least 2 hours.

6. Serve:

Fill glasses with ice cubes and pour the chilled tea over the ice. Garnish each glass with lemon and orange slices.

7. Enjoy:

Sip and savor the "I Love You Iced Tea" as you bask in the unique and delightful blend of flavors.

Nutrition Information:

(Per Serving)
- Calories: 80
- Total Fat: 0g
- Cholesterol: 0mg
- Sodium: 10mg
- Total Carbohydrates: 21g
- Dietary Fiber: 0g
- Sugars: 20g
- Protein: 0g

Indulge in this harmonious concoction that mirrors the diverse notes of Billie Eilish's music – a symphony of taste that's as refreshing as it is distinctive.

67. Oxytocin Orange Zest Cupcakes

Indulge your taste buds in a symphony of flavors with these Oxytocin Orange Zest Cupcakes—a delectable creation inspired by the sensational Billie Eilish. Just like Billie's music, these cupcakes are a harmonious blend of sweet and soulful. The infusion of oxytocin, often referred to as the "love hormone," brings an extra touch of warmth to these citrus-infused treats. Get ready to embark on a culinary journey that echoes the unique and vibrant spirit of Billie Eilish.

Serving: Makes 12 cupcakes
Preparation Time: 15 minutes
Ready Time: 30 minutes

Ingredients:
- 1 1/2 cups all-purpose flour
- 1 1/2 teaspoons baking powder
- 1/4 teaspoon baking soda
- 1/4 teaspoon salt
- 1/2 cup unsalted butter, softened
- 1 cup granulated sugar
- 2 large eggs
- 1 teaspoon vanilla extract
- 1/2 cup buttermilk
- Zest of 2 oranges
- 1/4 cup fresh orange juice

Instructions:
1. Preheat your oven to 350°F (175°C) and line a muffin tin with cupcake liners.
2. In a medium bowl, whisk together the flour, baking powder, baking soda, and salt. Set aside.
3. In a large bowl, cream together the softened butter and sugar until light and fluffy.
4. Add the eggs one at a time, beating well after each addition. Stir in the vanilla extract.
5. Gradually add the dry ingredients to the wet ingredients, alternating with the buttermilk. Begin and end with the dry ingredients, mixing until just combined.
6. Fold in the orange zest and fresh orange juice until evenly distributed throughout the batter.
7. Divide the batter evenly among the cupcake liners, filling each about two-thirds full.
8. Bake for 18-20 minutes or until a toothpick inserted into the center comes out clean.
9. Allow the cupcakes to cool in the tin for 5 minutes before transferring them to a wire rack to cool completely.

Nutrition Information:
Per serving (1 cupcake):
- Calories: 220
- Total Fat: 10g
- Saturated Fat: 6g
- Trans Fat: 0g
- Cholesterol: 55mg
- Sodium: 150mg
- Total Carbohydrates: 30g
- Dietary Fiber: 1g
- Sugars: 18g
- Protein: 3g

Savor the delightful combination of citrus and sweetness in each bite, and let the Oxytocin Orange Zest Cupcakes be a tribute to the enchanting creativity of Billie Eilish.

68. All The Good Girls Go To Hell Apricot Jam

'All The Good Girls Go To Hell Apricot Jam" is a delightful and unique jam inspired by the bold and eclectic style of the one and only Billie Eilish. This sweet and tangy apricot jam embodies the rebellious spirit that resonates with Billie's music. Whether you're a fan of her chart-topping hits or simply looking to add a touch of creativity to your breakfast spread, this jam is a perfect choice. Let the flavors of apricot and attitude collide in this delicious concoction.

Serving: This recipe makes approximately 2 cups of apricot jam.
Preparation Time: 15 minutes
Ready Time: 2 hours (including cooling time)

Ingredients:
- 2 cups fresh apricots, pitted and chopped
- 1 cup granulated sugar
- 2 tablespoons lemon juice
- 1 teaspoon vanilla extract
- 1/2 teaspoon ground cinnamon
- Pinch of salt

Instructions:

1. Prepare the Apricots:
- Wash and pit the fresh apricots, then chop them into small, uniform pieces.
2. Cooking the Jam:
- In a medium-sized saucepan, combine the chopped apricots, granulated sugar, lemon juice, vanilla extract, ground cinnamon, and a pinch of salt.
3. Cook Until Thickened:
- Over medium heat, bring the mixture to a boil, stirring occasionally. Once boiling, reduce the heat to low and let it simmer for about 15-20 minutes or until the mixture thickens.
4. Check the Consistency:
- To check if the jam has reached the desired consistency, place a small amount on a cold plate and let it sit for a minute. Run your finger through the jam, and if it wrinkles and holds its shape, it's ready.
5. Cooling and Storage:
- Remove the saucepan from heat and let the jam cool for 10-15 minutes. Pour it into sterilized jars, seal them, and let the jam cool to room temperature. Once cooled, refrigerate for at least 1-2 hours before serving.

Nutrition Information:

- *Serving Size:* 1 tablespoon
- *Calories:* 45
- *Total Fat:* 0g
- *Cholesterol:* 0mg
- *Sodium:* 1mg
- *Total Carbohydrates:* 11g
- *Dietary Fiber:* 0.5g
- *Sugars:* 10g
- *Protein:* 0.2g

Embrace the rebellious spirit of Billie Eilish with this "All The Good Girls Go To Hell Apricot Jam." Perfect for spreading on toast, pairing with cheeses, or adding a twist to your favorite desserts, this jam is a delectable celebration of music and flavor.

69. Not My Responsibility Napa Cabbage Salad

Embrace the unconventional with the "Not My Responsibility Napa Cabbage Salad," a dish inspired by the audacious and innovative spirit of Billie Eilish. Just like Billie's music, this salad is a harmonious blend of unexpected flavors and textures. Napa cabbage takes center stage in this recipe, offering a refreshing twist to your usual salad experience. Let the vibrant ingredients and unique combination in this dish remind you that creativity knows no bounds.

Serving: 4 servings
Preparation Time: 15 minutes
Ready Time: 15 minutes

Ingredients:
- 1 medium-sized Napa cabbage, finely shredded
- 1 cup cherry tomatoes, halved
- 1 cucumber, thinly sliced
- 1/2 red onion, thinly sliced
- 1/4 cup fresh cilantro, chopped
- 1/4 cup fresh mint leaves, torn
- 1/2 cup roasted sunflower seeds
- 1/2 cup feta cheese, crumbled
For the Dressing:
- 1/4 cup olive oil
- 2 tablespoons apple cider vinegar
- 1 tablespoon honey
- 1 teaspoon Dijon mustard
- Salt and pepper to taste

Instructions:
1. In a large bowl, combine the shredded Napa cabbage, cherry tomatoes, sliced cucumber, red onion, cilantro, mint leaves, sunflower seeds, and crumbled feta cheese.
2. In a small bowl, whisk together the olive oil, apple cider vinegar, honey, Dijon mustard, salt, and pepper to create the dressing.
3. Pour the dressing over the salad and toss until all ingredients are well-coated.
4. Allow the salad to sit for a few minutes to let the flavors meld together.

5. Serve the "Not My Responsibility Napa Cabbage Salad" on individual plates or in a large serving bowl.

Nutrition Information (per serving):
- Calories: 250
- Total Fat: 18g
- Saturated Fat: 5g
- Trans Fat: 0g
- Cholesterol: 20mg
- Sodium: 300mg
- Total Carbohydrates: 18g
- Dietary Fiber: 4g
- Sugars: 10g
- Protein: 6g
Note: Nutrition information is approximate and may vary based on specific ingredients used.

70. My Future Fennel Frittata

Indulge your taste buds in a symphony of flavors with "My Future Fennel Frittata," a culinary creation inspired by the eclectic and daring spirit of Billie Eilish. This frittata is a harmonious blend of vibrant ingredients that mirror the singer's dynamic personality. With a melody of fennel, eggs, and assorted herbs, this dish promises a taste experience that transcends the ordinary, just like Billie's music.

Serving: 4 servings
Preparation Time: 15 minutes
Ready Time: 35 minutes

Ingredients:
- 6 large eggs
- 1 cup fennel bulb, thinly sliced
- 1/2 cup red bell pepper, diced
- 1/2 cup cherry tomatoes, halved
- 1/4 cup fresh parsley, chopped
- 1/4 cup fresh chives, chopped
- 1/2 cup feta cheese, crumbled

- 2 tablespoons olive oil
- Salt and pepper to taste

Instructions:
1. Preheat the Oven:
Preheat your oven to 375°F (190°C).
2. Sauté Fennel and Bell Pepper:
In an oven-safe skillet, heat olive oil over medium heat. Add sliced fennel and diced red bell pepper. Sauté until fennel is tender, about 5 minutes.
3. Prepare Egg Mixture:
In a bowl, whisk together eggs, salt, and pepper. Add chopped parsley and chives, mixing well.
4. Combine Ingredients:
Pour the egg mixture over the sautéed fennel and bell pepper in the skillet. Sprinkle halved cherry tomatoes and crumbled feta evenly over the eggs.
5. Bake:
Transfer the skillet to the preheated oven and bake for approximately 20-25 minutes or until the frittata is set and the top is golden brown.
6. Garnish and Serve:
Once baked, remove from the oven and let it cool for a few minutes. Garnish with additional fresh herbs if desired. Slice into wedges and serve.

Nutrition Information:
(Per Serving)
- Calories: 220
- Total Fat: 16g
- Saturated Fat: 5g
- Cholesterol: 280mg
- Sodium: 350mg
- Total Carbohydrates: 6g
- Dietary Fiber: 2g
- Sugars: 3g
- Protein: 12g

Elevate your breakfast or brunch experience with this Future Fennel Frittata, a dish that captures the essence of Billie Eilish's bold creativity in every bite. Enjoy the fusion of fresh ingredients and vibrant flavors that harmonize to create a symphony on your palate.

71. Therefore I Am Tangerine Tiramisu

Indulge your taste buds in a symphony of flavors with the "Therefore I Am Tangerine Tiramisu," a delightful dessert inspired by the bold and eclectic style of the one and only Billie Eilish. This fusion of citrusy tangerine and the classic Italian tiramisu will take you on a culinary journey, just like Billie's genre-defying music. Prepare to savor every note of this harmonious treat!

Serving: Serves 8
Preparation Time: 20 minutes
Ready Time: Chill for at least 4 hours or overnight

Ingredients:
- 1 cup strong brewed coffee, cooled
- 1/4 cup tangerine juice
- 1 tablespoon orange liqueur (optional)
- 3 large egg yolks
- 1 cup granulated sugar
- 1 1/2 cups mascarpone cheese, softened
- 1 cup heavy cream
- 1 teaspoon vanilla extract
- Zest of 2 tangerines
- 24 to 30 ladyfinger cookies
- Cocoa powder for dusting

Instructions:
1. In a shallow dish, combine the brewed coffee, tangerine juice, and orange liqueur. Set aside.
2. In a heatproof bowl, whisk together the egg yolks and sugar. Place the bowl over a pot of simmering water, creating a double boiler. Whisk continuously until the mixture becomes pale and slightly thickened.
3. Remove the bowl from heat and let it cool for a few minutes. Add the mascarpone cheese and mix until smooth.
4. In a separate bowl, whip the heavy cream and vanilla extract until stiff peaks form.
5. Gently fold the whipped cream into the mascarpone mixture until well combined. Add the tangerine zest and fold until incorporated.

6. Dip each ladyfinger into the coffee-tangerine mixture, ensuring they are soaked but not overly saturated. Arrange a layer of dipped ladyfingers in the bottom of a serving dish.
7. Spread half of the mascarpone mixture over the ladyfingers, creating an even layer.
8. Repeat the process with another layer of dipped ladyfingers and the remaining mascarpone mixture.
9. Cover and refrigerate the tiramisu for at least 4 hours or overnight to allow the flavors to meld.
10. Before serving, dust the top with cocoa powder for a finishing touch.

Nutrition Information:
(Per serving)
- Calories: 380
- Total Fat: 25g
- Saturated Fat: 15g
- Cholesterol: 150mg
- Sodium: 35mg
- Total Carbohydrates: 33g
- Dietary Fiber: 1g
- Sugars: 20g
- Protein: 6g

Immerse yourself in the unique combination of tangerine and tiramisu – a dessert as bold and unforgettable as the music that inspired it.

72. Getting Older Green Grape Gazpacho

As the years go by, flavors evolve, and this "Getting Older Green Grape Gazpacho" embodies that progression perfectly. Inspired by Billie Eilish's creative journey and her ever-evolving style, this gazpacho celebrates change and growth with a vibrant blend of flavors and textures that mature gracefully with time.

Serving: 4 servings
Preparation time: 15 minutes
Ready time: 1 hour (chilled)

Ingredients:

- 2 cups green grapes, halved and deseeded
- 1 cucumber, peeled and chopped
- 1 green bell pepper, seeded and diced
- 2 green onions, chopped
- 2 cloves garlic, minced
- 1 jalapeño pepper, seeded and chopped
- 2 cups baby spinach
- 1/4 cup fresh parsley, chopped
- 1/4 cup fresh cilantro, chopped
- 2 tablespoons lime juice
- 2 tablespoons white wine vinegar
- 1/4 cup extra-virgin olive oil
- Salt and pepper to taste
- 1 cup cold water (adjust for desired consistency)

Instructions:

1. In a blender, combine the green grapes, cucumber, green bell pepper, green onions, garlic, jalapeño pepper, baby spinach, parsley, cilantro, lime juice, and white wine vinegar.
2. Blend the mixture until smooth, gradually adding the olive oil while the blender is running.
3. Season the gazpacho with salt and pepper to taste, and adjust the consistency by adding cold water as needed.
4. Refrigerate the gazpacho for at least an hour to chill and allow the flavors to meld together.
5. Before serving, give the gazpacho a gentle stir. Garnish with a few slices of green grapes, a sprig of parsley, or a drizzle of olive oil if desired.

Nutrition Information (per serving):

- Calories: 180
- Total Fat: 14g
- Saturated Fat: 2g
- Cholesterol: 0mg
- Sodium: 20mg
- Total Carbohydrate: 14g
- Dietary Fiber: 3g
- Sugars: 8g
- Protein: 2g

This gazpacho not only celebrates the changing flavors of time but also provides a refreshing, nutritious addition to any meal. It's a testament to growth and evolution, much like the journey of Billie Eilish herself.

73. Overheated Olive Oil Dip

Inspired by Billie Eilish's fiery energy, the Overheated Olive Oil Dip captures the boldness of her music in a tantalizing, spicy dip. This recipe brings together the richness of olive oil and the heat of red pepper flakes for a flavor explosion that's perfect for sharing with friends and family.

Serving: 4-6 people
Preparation time: 5 minutes
Ready time: 10 minutes

Ingredients:
- 1 cup extra virgin olive oil
- 2 cloves garlic, thinly sliced
- 1 teaspoon red pepper flakes (adjust to taste)
- 1 teaspoon dried oregano
- 1 teaspoon dried basil
- 1 teaspoon dried thyme
- Salt and black pepper to taste
- Zest of 1 lemon
- 1 tablespoon chopped fresh parsley (for garnish)
- Slices of crusty bread, for serving

Instructions:
1. Heat the olive oil in a small saucepan over low-medium heat.
2. Add the thinly sliced garlic to the oil and let it cook gently until it begins to turn golden brown, about 2-3 minutes.
3. Stir in the red pepper flakes, dried oregano, basil, and thyme. Let the mixture simmer for an additional 2-3 minutes, ensuring the flavors infuse into the oil.
4. Season with salt and black pepper according to your taste. Stir in the lemon zest for a citrusy lift.
5. Remove the saucepan from heat and transfer the spicy oil to a serving dish.

6. Garnish with chopped fresh parsley for a burst of color and freshness.
7. Serve the overheated olive oil dip warm with slices of crusty bread for dipping.

Nutrition Information: (approximate per serving)
- Calories: 240
- Total Fat: 27g
- Saturated Fat: 4g
- Trans Fat: 0g
- Sodium: 110mg
- Total Carbohydrates: 1g
- Dietary Fiber: 0.5g
- Sugars: 0g
- Protein: 0.5g

Enjoy the zesty and spicy kick of this dip while indulging in the music of Billie Eilish—let it be the soundtrack to your flavorful moments!

74. Your Power Yellow Pepper Pesto

This vibrant yellow pepper pesto encapsulates the vivid energy of Billie Eilish's music. Bursting with flavors and a zesty punch, it's a versatile sauce that adds a unique twist to any dish. Whether slathered over pasta or used as a dip, this power-packed pesto is bound to elevate your culinary experience.

Serving: 4 servings
Preparation time: 15 minutes
Ready time: 20 minutes

Ingredients:
- 2 yellow bell peppers, roasted and peeled
- 1/2 cup fresh basil leaves
- 1/3 cup grated Parmesan cheese
- 1/4 cup pine nuts, toasted
- 2 cloves garlic, minced
- 1/4 cup extra-virgin olive oil
- Salt and pepper to taste

Instructions:
1. Roast the Peppers: Preheat your oven's broiler. Place the whole yellow bell peppers on a baking sheet and broil, turning occasionally, until the skins are charred and blistered, about 10-15 minutes. Transfer the peppers to a bowl, cover with plastic wrap, and let them cool. Once cooled, peel off the skins, remove seeds and stems, and roughly chop the peppers.
2. Prepare the Pesto Base: In a food processor, combine the roasted yellow peppers, basil leaves, grated Parmesan cheese, toasted pine nuts, and minced garlic. Pulse until the ingredients are finely chopped and combined.
3. Add Olive Oil: While the processor is running, slowly drizzle in the olive oil until the mixture forms a smooth, vibrant pesto. Season with salt and pepper to taste.
4. Adjust Consistency and Taste: If the pesto seems too thick, add a bit more olive oil. Taste and adjust seasoning as needed.
5. Serve or Store: Use immediately as a sauce for pasta, a spread on sandwiches, or a dip for veggies. Store any leftover pesto in an airtight container in the refrigerator for up to a week.

Nutrition Information (per serving):
- Calories: 220
- Total Fat: 20g
- Saturated Fat: 3.5g
- Cholesterol: 5mg
- Sodium: 160mg
- Total Carbohydrate: 6g
- Dietary Fiber: 2g
- Sugars: 3g
- Protein: 5g

This "Your Power Yellow Pepper Pesto" is a celebration of bold flavors and versatility, echoing the artistic depth of Billie Eilish's music. Enjoy its zesty essence and vibrant hue as it enhances your culinary creations!

75. My Strange Addiction Maple Syrup Pancakes

Indulge your taste buds in a symphony of flavors with "My Strange Addiction Maple Syrup Pancakes." Inspired by the unique and eclectic palette of Billie Eilish, this pancake recipe takes breakfast to a whole new level. The rich warmth of maple syrup intertwines with the fluffy texture of the pancakes, creating a melody of taste that's both comforting and extraordinary. Get ready to embark on a culinary journey that mirrors Billie's distinct style – bold, unexpected, and utterly delicious.

Serving: 4 servings
Preparation Time: 15 minutes
Ready Time: 30 minutes

Ingredients:
- 1 cup all-purpose flour
- 2 tablespoons sugar
- 1 teaspoon baking powder
- 1/2 teaspoon baking soda
- 1/4 teaspoon salt
- 3/4 cup buttermilk
- 1/4 cup milk
- 1 large egg
- 2 tablespoons unsalted butter, melted
- 1 teaspoon vanilla extract
- 1/3 cup maple syrup (plus extra for serving)
- Cooking spray or additional butter for greasing the pan

Instructions:
1. Prepare the Batter:
In a large mixing bowl, whisk together the flour, sugar, baking powder, baking soda, and salt.
2. Mix Wet Ingredients:
In a separate bowl, combine the buttermilk, milk, egg, melted butter, and vanilla extract. Mix well until the wet ingredients are thoroughly combined.
3. Combine Wet and Dry Ingredients:
Pour the wet ingredients into the bowl with the dry ingredients. Stir until just combined, being careful not to overmix. It's okay if the batter has a few lumps.
4. Cook the Pancakes:
Heat a griddle or non-stick skillet over medium heat and lightly coat with cooking spray or butter. Pour 1/4 cup portions of batter onto the griddle

for each pancake. Cook until bubbles form on the surface, then flip and cook until golden brown on the other side.

5. Serve:

Stack the pancakes on a plate and drizzle with maple syrup. For an extra touch inspired by Billie Eilish, you can add a sprinkle of edible glitter or your favorite colorful toppings.

Nutrition Information:

Note: Nutrition information is approximate and may vary based on specific ingredients used.

- Calories: 280 per serving
- Total Fat: 8g
- Saturated Fat: 4g
- Trans Fat: 0g
- Cholesterol: 55mg
- Sodium: 480mg
- Total Carbohydrates: 45g
- Dietary Fiber: 1g
- Sugars: 16g
- Protein: 6g

Enjoy your "My Strange Addiction Maple Syrup Pancakes" – a harmonious blend of flavors that pays homage to Billie Eilish's one-of-a-kind style.

76. Goldwing Grapefruit Granita

Indulge your taste buds with the electrifying harmony of flavors in our "Goldwing Grapefruit Granita," a sensational treat inspired by the bold and vibrant spirit of Billie Eilish. This refreshing and tangy granita captures the essence of Billie's eclectic style, offering a burst of citrusy goodness that's as unique as her musical artistry. Immerse yourself in the cool embrace of this frozen delight and experience the symphony of taste that mirrors Billie's one-of-a-kind creativity.

Serving: Serves 4
Preparation Time: 15 minutes
Ready Time: 4 hours (including freezing time)

Ingredients:
- 2 large ruby red grapefruits, juiced
- 1/2 cup goldwing honey (or any preferred honey)
- 1/4 cup water
- 2 tablespoons freshly squeezed lemon juice
- Zest of 1 grapefruit
- 1/4 cup sugar (adjust to taste)
- Mint leaves for garnish (optional)

Instructions:
1. In a saucepan over medium heat, combine goldwing honey, water, and sugar. Stir until the sugar dissolves, creating a simple syrup. Remove from heat and let it cool to room temperature.
2. In a mixing bowl, combine the freshly squeezed grapefruit juice, lemon juice, and grapefruit zest.
3. Gradually pour the cooled honey syrup into the juice mixture, stirring gently to ensure even blending.
4. Taste the mixture and adjust the sweetness if necessary by adding more honey or sugar.
5. Pour the mixture into a shallow dish, ensuring an even layer. Place the dish in the freezer.
6. Every 30 minutes, use a fork to fluff the mixture, breaking up any ice crystals. Repeat this process for about 3-4 hours, or until the granita reaches a slushy consistency.
7. Once the granita is fully frozen and fluffed, scoop it into serving glasses.
8. Garnish with fresh mint leaves for an extra burst of flavor and aroma.
9. Serve immediately and enjoy the zesty, frozen bliss of Goldwing Grapefruit Granita!

Nutrition Information:
(Per Serving)
- Calories: 120
- Total Fat: 0g
- Cholesterol: 0mg
- Sodium: 2mg
- Total Carbohydrates: 31g
- Dietary Fiber: 1g
- Sugars: 27g
- Protein: 1g

Note: Nutrition information is approximate and may vary based on specific ingredients used.

77. All The Good Girls Go To Hell Asparagus Spears

Indulge your taste buds in the rebellious and flavorful world of Billie Eilish with these "All The Good Girls Go To Hell Asparagus Spears." Inspired by the eclectic and bold spirit of the artist, this dish promises a symphony of textures and tastes that will leave your senses tingling. Whether you're a devoted fan or simply seeking a culinary adventure, these asparagus spears are a perfect ode to Billie's unique style.

Serving: Serves 4
Preparation Time: 15 minutes
Ready Time: 25 minutes

Ingredients:
- 1 bunch fresh asparagus spears
- 2 tablespoons olive oil
- 2 cloves garlic, minced
- 1 teaspoon chili flakes (adjust according to spice preference)
- Salt and pepper to taste
- Zest of one lemon
- 1 tablespoon fresh parsley, finely chopped (for garnish)

Instructions:
1. Preheat the Oven:
- Preheat your oven to 400°F (200°C).
2. Prepare the Asparagus:
- Wash the asparagus spears thoroughly and trim the tough ends.
3. Season the Asparagus:
- In a mixing bowl, toss the asparagus with olive oil, minced garlic, chili flakes, salt, and pepper. Ensure the asparagus is evenly coated.
4. Arrange on Baking Sheet:
- Place the seasoned asparagus spears on a baking sheet in a single layer.
5. Roast in the Oven:
- Roast in the preheated oven for 10-12 minutes or until the asparagus is tender, with a slight crispiness.

6. Add Zest:
- Once out of the oven, sprinkle lemon zest over the roasted asparagus for a burst of citrusy freshness.
7. Garnish:
- Transfer the asparagus to a serving platter and garnish with freshly chopped parsley.
8. Serve:
- Serve these "All The Good Girls Go To Hell Asparagus Spears" as a vibrant side dish that complements any main course or enjoy them as a standalone snack.

Nutrition Information:
- *Note: Nutritional values are approximate and may vary based on specific ingredients used.*
- Calories per serving: 80
- Total Fat: 6g
- Saturated Fat: 1g
- Cholesterol: 0mg
- Sodium: 150mg
- Total Carbohydrates: 7g
- Dietary Fiber: 4g
- Sugars: 2g
- Protein: 4g

Embrace the rebellious flavors of Billie Eilish with these asparagus spears that are bound to take your taste buds on a thrilling ride. Whether you're hosting a dinner party or simply treating yourself, these spears are a delightful addition to any occasion.

78. NDA Nutmeg Muffins

Indulge your taste buds in the harmonious symphony of flavors with our NDA Nutmeg Muffins, inspired by the enigmatic Billie Eilish. These muffins encapsulate the essence of Billie's eclectic style and unique persona. The subtle warmth of nutmeg paired with a clandestine blend of ingredients makes these muffins a delectable treat that resonates with the artist's mysterious allure. Get ready to embark on a culinary journey that mirrors Billie's creativity and originality.

Serving: 12 muffins
Preparation time: 15 minutes
Ready time: 30 minutes

Ingredients:
- 2 cups all-purpose flour
- 1 cup granulated sugar
- 1 tablespoon baking powder
- 1/2 teaspoon salt
- 1/2 teaspoon ground nutmeg
- 1 cup milk
- 1/2 cup unsalted butter, melted
- 2 large eggs
- 1 teaspoon vanilla extract
- 1/2 cup NDA (Nutmeg, Date, and Almond) blend:
- 1/4 cup chopped dates
- 1/4 cup chopped almonds

Instructions:
1. Preheat your oven to 375°F (190°C) and line a muffin tin with paper liners.
2. In a large mixing bowl, whisk together the flour, sugar, baking powder, salt, and ground nutmeg.
3. In a separate bowl, combine the milk, melted butter, eggs, and vanilla extract. Mix well.
4. Pour the wet ingredients into the dry ingredients, stirring until just combined. Be careful not to overmix; a few lumps are okay.
5. Gently fold in the NDA blend – chopped dates and almonds. This adds a delightful texture and a hint of sweetness.
6. Spoon the batter into the prepared muffin tin, filling each cup about two-thirds full.
7. Bake for 18-20 minutes or until a toothpick inserted into the center comes out clean.
8. Allow the muffins to cool in the tin for 5 minutes before transferring them to a wire rack to cool completely.

Nutrition Information (per serving):
- Calories: 220
- Total Fat: 9g
- Saturated Fat: 5g

- Trans Fat: 0g
- Cholesterol: 50mg
- Sodium: 220mg
- Total Carbohydrates: 31g
- Dietary Fiber: 1g
- Sugars: 16g
- Protein: 4g

Note: Nutrition information is approximate and may vary based on specific ingredients used.

79. Therefore I Am Truffle Tater Tots

Indulge your taste buds in a symphony of flavors with the "Therefore I Am Truffle Tater Tots," a dish inspired by the iconic Billie Eilish. This culinary creation mirrors Billie's bold and eclectic style, combining the humble tater tot with the decadence of truffle, resulting in a snack that's as audacious as it is delicious.

Serving: Serves 4
Preparation Time: 15 minutes
Ready Time: 30 minutes

Ingredients:
- 2 pounds frozen tater tots
- 2 tablespoons truffle oil
- 1/4 cup grated Parmesan cheese
- 1 teaspoon garlic powder
- 1/2 teaspoon onion powder
- Salt and black pepper to taste
- Fresh parsley, chopped (for garnish)

Instructions:
1. Preheat the Oven:
Preheat your oven according to the instructions on the tater tots package.
2. Bake the Tater Tots:
Arrange the frozen tater tots in a single layer on a baking sheet. Bake them in the preheated oven until they are golden brown and crispy, following the recommended time on the package.

3. Truffle Infusion:

While the tater tots are baking, in a small bowl, mix together the truffle oil, grated Parmesan cheese, garlic powder, onion powder, salt, and black pepper.

4. Truffle Toss:

Once the tater tots are out of the oven and still hot, transfer them to a large bowl. Drizzle the truffle oil mixture over the tots and gently toss until they are evenly coated.

5. Garnish:

Sprinkle the truffle-infused tater tots with fresh chopped parsley for an extra burst of freshness and color.

6. Serve:

Plate the "Therefore I Am Truffle Tater Tots" on a stylish dish and serve them hot. These tots are perfect for sharing with friends or enjoying as a solo treat.

Nutrition Information:

Note: Nutritional values are approximate and may vary based on specific brands and quantities used.

- Calories: 300 per serving
- Total Fat: 15g
- Saturated Fat: 3g
- Trans Fat: 0g
- Cholesterol: 5mg
- Sodium: 650mg
- Total Carbohydrates: 35g
- Dietary Fiber: 3g
- Sugars: 0g
- Protein: 5g

Elevate your snack game with these truffle-infused tater tots inspired by Billie Eilish, and let the bold flavors take you on a culinary journey like no other.

80. I Love You Iceberg Lettuce Wraps

These "I Love You Iceberg Lettuce Wraps" are a delightful culinary tribute to the iconic Billie Eilish, capturing the essence of her soulful music and unique style. Inspired by the artist's love for fresh, crisp ingredients, these wraps are a perfect blend of simplicity and flavor. The crisp iceberg lettuce serves as a wholesome vessel for a medley of vibrant and nutritious fillings, creating a dish that's as pleasing to the palate as Billie's music is to the ears.

Serving: 4 servings
Preparation Time: 15 minutes
Ready Time: 15 minutes

Ingredients:
- 1 pound ground turkey or chicken
- 1 tablespoon olive oil
- 1 small onion, finely diced
- 2 cloves garlic, minced
- 1 teaspoon ground cumin
- 1 teaspoon chili powder
- Salt and pepper, to taste
- 1 cup corn kernels (fresh or frozen)
- 1 cup black beans, drained and rinsed
- 1 cup cherry tomatoes, diced
- 1 avocado, diced
- 1/2 cup fresh cilantro, chopped
- Juice of 1 lime
- 1 head iceberg lettuce, leaves separated

Instructions:
1. In a large skillet, heat olive oil over medium heat. Add diced onions and minced garlic, sautéing until softened.
2. Add ground turkey or chicken to the skillet, breaking it apart with a spoon. Cook until browned and cooked through.
3. Season the meat with ground cumin, chili powder, salt, and pepper. Stir well to incorporate the spices.
4. Add corn kernels and black beans to the skillet, cooking for an additional 3-5 minutes until heated through.
5. Remove the skillet from heat and stir in diced cherry tomatoes, avocado, fresh cilantro, and lime juice. Mix gently to combine.
6. Carefully separate the leaves of the iceberg lettuce to create cups for the filling.
7. Spoon the turkey or chicken mixture into each lettuce cup, distributing the filling evenly.

8. Serve the "I Love You Iceberg Lettuce Wraps" on a platter, allowing guests to customize their wraps with additional toppings like salsa, guacamole, or sour cream if desired.

Nutrition Information:
Note: Nutrition information is approximate and may vary based on specific ingredients used.
- Calories per serving: 320
- Protein: 22g
- Carbohydrates: 22g
- Fiber: 8g
- Sugar: 4g
- Fat: 18g
- Saturated Fat: 3g
- Cholesterol: 50mg
- Sodium: 480mg

These wraps are a harmonious medley of textures and flavors, embodying the spirit of Billie Eilish's eclectic musical journey. Enjoy the freshness and love packed into each bite!

81. Lost Cause Lemon Lollipop

Indulge your taste buds in the rebellious spirit of Billie Eilish with our "Lost Cause Lemon Lollipop" recipe. This zesty and sweet treat captures the essence of Billie's iconic song, "Lost Cause," in a delightful lemon-flavored lollipop that's as bold and unforgettable as the artist herself. Get ready to savor the flavors of this unique culinary creation inspired by the musical genius of Billie Eilish.

Serving: Makes 12 lollipops
Preparation Time: 15 minutes
Ready Time: 2 hours (including chilling time)

Ingredients:
- 2 cups granulated sugar
- 2/3 cup water
- 1/2 cup corn syrup
- 1 tablespoon lemon zest

- 1/4 cup fresh lemon juice
- 1/4 teaspoon yellow food coloring (optional)
- Lollipop sticks

Instructions:
1. Prepare Equipment:
Line a baking sheet with parchment paper and place lollipop sticks on it, spacing them apart.
2. Create Sugar Syrup:
In a medium saucepan over medium heat, combine sugar, water, and corn syrup. Stir until the sugar dissolves, then stop stirring and let the mixture come to a boil.
3. Cook to Desired Temperature:
Use a candy thermometer to monitor the temperature. Cook the mixture until it reaches 300°F (hard crack stage). This usually takes about 10 minutes.
4. Add Lemon Flavor:
Remove the saucepan from heat and carefully stir in lemon zest, lemon juice, and yellow food coloring (if using). Be cautious, as the mixture will bubble when the lemon juice is added.
5. Form Lollipops:
Quickly spoon the hot mixture onto the prepared baking sheet over each lollipop stick. Allow the lollipops to cool and harden.
6. Chill:
Place the baking sheet in the refrigerator for at least 1-2 hours or until the lollipops are completely set.
7. Enjoy:
Once set, remove the lollipops from the refrigerator and enjoy the vibrant and tangy flavor of your Lost Cause Lemon Lollipops.

Nutrition Information:
(Per serving - 1 lollipop)
- Calories: 160
- Total Fat: 0g
- Cholesterol: 0mg
- Sodium: 5mg
- Total Carbohydrates: 42g
- Sugars: 42g
- Protein: 0g

Immerse yourself in the world of Billie Eilish with these Lost Cause Lemon Lollipops, a delectable tribute to her bold and unique style.

82. Ocean Eyes Oregano Orzo

'Ocean Eyes Oregano Orzo" is a delightful pasta dish inspired by the soulful and ethereal vibes of Billie Eilish's music. Named after her iconic song "Ocean Eyes," this recipe combines the freshness of the ocean with the aromatic allure of oregano, creating a harmonious symphony of flavors.

Serving: 4 servings
Preparation Time: 15 minutes
Ready Time: 25 minutes

Ingredients:
- 2 cups orzo pasta
- 1 lb fresh shrimp, peeled and deveined
- 1 cup cherry tomatoes, halved
- 1/2 cup Kalamata olives, pitted and sliced
- 1/4 cup fresh parsley, chopped
- 4 cloves garlic, minced
- 1/3 cup extra virgin olive oil
- 2 tablespoons fresh lemon juice
- 1 teaspoon dried oregano
- Salt and pepper to taste
- Grated Parmesan cheese for garnish (optional)

Instructions:
1. Cook the Orzo:
- Bring a large pot of salted water to a boil.
- Cook the orzo according to the package instructions until al dente.
- Drain and set aside.
2. Prepare the Shrimp:
- In a large skillet, heat olive oil over medium heat.
- Add minced garlic and sauté until fragrant.
- Add shrimp and cook until they turn pink and opaque.
- Season with salt, pepper, and dried oregano.

- Remove the shrimp from the skillet and set aside.
3. Combine Ingredients:
- In the same skillet, add cooked orzo, cherry tomatoes, Kalamata olives, and fresh parsley.
- Drizzle with fresh lemon juice and toss to combine.
- Add the cooked shrimp back to the skillet and gently mix.
4. Garnish and Serve:
- Garnish with additional fresh parsley and grated Parmesan cheese if desired.
- Serve hot, allowing the flavors to meld together beautifully.

Nutrition Information:
(Per Serving)
- Calories: 450
- Total Fat: 20g
- Saturated Fat: 3g
- Cholesterol: 120mg
- Sodium: 480mg
- Total Carbohydrates: 50g
- Dietary Fiber: 3g
- Sugars: 2g
- Protein: 20g
Note:
Feel free to customize this dish with your favorite seafood or additional vegetables to make it uniquely yours. "Ocean Eyes Oregano Orzo" is a celebration of Billie Eilish's artistry, and we hope it brings a symphony of flavors to your table. Enjoy!

83. Oxytocin Orange Oat Bars

Billie Eilish's music is a symphony of emotions, and her eclectic style is an inspiration in itself. These "Oxytocin Orange Oat Bars" are a delightful representation of the warmth and positivity that Billie's music brings. Packed with wholesome ingredients, these bars are not only a treat for your taste buds but also a boost for your mood.

Serving: Makes 12 bars
Preparation Time: 15 minutes

Ready Time: 45 minutes

Ingredients:
- 2 cups old-fashioned oats
- 1 cup almond flour
- 1/2 cup shredded coconut
- 1/2 cup chopped almonds
- 1/2 cup dried cranberries
- Zest of 1 orange
- 1/2 teaspoon salt
- 1/2 cup coconut oil, melted
- 1/2 cup honey or maple syrup
- 1 teaspoon vanilla extract
- 1/4 cup dark chocolate chips (optional, for drizzling)

Instructions:
1. Preheat the oven to 350°F (175°C). Line a 9x9-inch baking pan with parchment paper, leaving some overhang for easy removal.
2. In a large mixing bowl, combine the oats, almond flour, shredded coconut, chopped almonds, dried cranberries, orange zest, and salt.
3. In a separate bowl, whisk together the melted coconut oil, honey or maple syrup, and vanilla extract.
4. Pour the wet ingredients over the dry ingredients and mix until well combined.
5. Press the mixture firmly into the prepared baking pan, creating an even layer.
6. Bake in the preheated oven for 25-30 minutes or until the edges turn golden brown.
7. Allow the bars to cool completely in the pan before using the parchment paper overhang to lift them out.
8. Optional: Melt the dark chocolate chips and drizzle over the cooled bars for an extra touch of sweetness.
9. Once the chocolate has set, cut the bars into 12 squares.

Nutrition Information:
(Per serving)
- Calories: 240
- Total Fat: 14g
- Saturated Fat: 8g
- Trans Fat: 0g

- Cholesterol: 0mg
- Sodium: 80mg
- Total Carbohydrates: 26g
- Dietary Fiber: 4g
- Sugars: 14g
- Protein: 4g

Enjoy these Oxytocin Orange Oat Bars as a snack or dessert, and let the positive vibes flow with every bite!

84. My Future Mango Mousse

Embark on a flavorful journey with "My Future Mango Mousse," a delectable dessert inspired by the artistic genius, Billie Eilish. Just like her music, this mango mousse is a harmonious blend of sweet and soulful, promising to transport you to a world of pure indulgence. Treat your taste buds to this smooth and velvety creation that's as unique as Billie's musical style.

Serving: 4 servings
Preparation Time: 20 minutes
Ready Time: 4 hours (including chilling time)

Ingredients:
- 2 ripe mangoes, peeled and diced
- 1/2 cup granulated sugar
- 1 tablespoon lemon juice
- 1 teaspoon gelatin
- 2 tablespoons water
- 1 cup heavy cream
- 1 teaspoon vanilla extract
- Fresh mint leaves for garnish (optional)

Instructions:
1. Prepare the Mango Puree:
- In a blender, combine the diced mangoes, sugar, and lemon juice. Blend until you achieve a smooth puree. Set aside.
2. Bloom the Gelatin:

- In a small bowl, mix the gelatin with water. Allow it to sit for a few minutes until it blooms.
3. Heat the Gelatin:
- Gently heat the bloomed gelatin in a microwave or on the stovetop until it dissolves completely. Be cautious not to overheat.
4. Incorporate Gelatin into Mango Puree:
- Add the dissolved gelatin to the mango puree and blend until well combined.
5. Whip the Heavy Cream:
- In a separate bowl, whip the heavy cream and vanilla extract until stiff peaks form.
6. Fold in the Whipped Cream:
- Gently fold the whipped cream into the mango mixture until you achieve a uniform, airy texture.
7. Chill the Mousse:
- Divide the mousse into serving glasses or bowls. Refrigerate for at least 4 hours, or until the mousse is set.
8. Garnish and Serve:
- Before serving, garnish with fresh mint leaves if desired. The mousse is now ready to be enjoyed!

Nutrition Information:
- *(Per Serving)*
- Calories: 280
- Total Fat: 18g
- Saturated Fat: 11g
- Cholesterol: 65mg
- Sodium: 30mg
- Total Carbohydrates: 28g
- Dietary Fiber: 2g
- Sugars: 25g
- Protein: 2g

Indulge in the musical and culinary artistry inspired by Billie Eilish with "My Future Mango Mousse." This dessert is a symphony of flavors that will leave your senses singing.

85. Everybody Dies Edamame Dip

Embrace the enigmatic world of Billie Eilish with the "Everybody Dies Edamame Dip," a spellbinding concoction inspired by the artist's distinctive style and fearless spirit. This vibrant edamame dip is a testament to the creativity and uniqueness that defines Billie's musical journey. So, gather your ingredients and get ready to experience a taste as bold and unforgettable as Billie herself.

Serving: Makes approximately 2 cups of dip.
Preparation Time: 15 minutes
Ready Time: 15 minutes

Ingredients:
- 2 cups shelled edamame, cooked and cooled
- 1/4 cup fresh cilantro, chopped
- 1/4 cup tahini
- 2 cloves garlic, minced
- 1/4 cup extra virgin olive oil
- 2 tablespoons fresh lemon juice
- 1 teaspoon ground cumin
- 1/2 teaspoon salt
- 1/4 teaspoon black pepper
- Optional: red pepper flakes for a spicy kick

Instructions:
1. Prepare Edamame: Cook the shelled edamame according to package instructions. Once cooked, drain and let them cool to room temperature.
2. Blend Ingredients: In a food processor, combine the cooled edamame, cilantro, tahini, minced garlic, olive oil, lemon juice, ground cumin, salt, and black pepper. If you like a bit of heat, add red pepper flakes to taste.
3. Blend Until Smooth: Process the mixture until smooth and creamy. If the dip is too thick, you can add a bit more olive oil or water to achieve your desired consistency.
4. Taste and Adjust: Taste the dip and adjust the seasoning if necessary. Add more salt, pepper, or lemon juice to suit your preferences.
5. Serve: Transfer the edamame dip to a serving bowl. Garnish with additional cilantro and a drizzle of olive oil if desired.
6. Enjoy: Serve with your favorite crackers, pita bread, or fresh vegetable sticks. This dip is perfect for gatherings, parties, or a solo indulgence while you immerse yourself in the music of Billie Eilish.

Nutrition Information:
Note: Nutritional values are approximate and may vary based on specific ingredients used.
- Calories per serving: 120
- Total Fat: 9g
- Saturated Fat: 1g
- Trans Fat: 0g
- Cholesterol: 0mg
- Sodium: 200mg
- Total Carbohydrates: 7g
- Dietary Fiber: 3g
- Sugars: 1g
- Protein: 5g

Feel the electric vibes of Billie Eilish as you savor the "Everybody Dies Edamame Dip." This culinary creation is a tribute to the bold and unconventional, just like the music that inspired it. Enjoy the journey of flavors and emotions that unfold with every delightful scoop.

86. Goldwing Grilled Grapefruit

Inspired by Billie Eilish's eclectic style and bold creativity, the Goldwing Grilled Grapefruit is a vibrant and unconventional twist on a classic fruit. This dish reflects the artist's love for uniqueness and unexpected combinations. The warmth of the grill enhances the natural sweetness of grapefruit, creating a delightful sensory experience that mirrors Billie's ability to surprise and captivate.

Serving: Serves 4
Preparation Time: 15 minutes
Ready Time: 20 minutes

Ingredients:
- 2 large ruby red grapefruits
- 2 tablespoons honey
- 1 tablespoon olive oil
- 1 teaspoon ground cinnamon
- A pinch of sea salt
- Fresh mint leaves for garnish (optional)

Instructions:
1. Preheat the Grill:
- Preheat your grill to medium-high heat.
2. Prepare the Grapefruits:
- Cut the grapefruits in half, and using a sharp knife, carefully segment each half by cutting along the membranes. This will make it easier to eat later.
3. Create the Marinade:
- In a small bowl, whisk together honey, olive oil, ground cinnamon, and a pinch of sea salt. This creates a sweet and savory marinade.
4. Marinate the Grapefruits:
- Brush the cut side of each grapefruit half with the prepared marinade, ensuring an even coating.
5. Grill the Grapefruits:
- Place the grapefruit halves, cut side down, on the preheated grill. Cook for about 2-3 minutes or until grill marks appear and the fruit is slightly caramelized.
6. Serve:
- Remove the grilled grapefruits from the grill and arrange them on a serving platter. Drizzle any remaining marinade over the top.
7. Garnish (Optional):
- Garnish with fresh mint leaves for a burst of color and added freshness.
8. Enjoy:
- Serve the Goldwing Grilled Grapefruit immediately while still warm. The combination of the smoky flavor from the grill and the sweet-tartness of the fruit is a unique and delightful experience.

Nutrition Information:
(Per Serving)
- Calories: 120
- Total Fat: 4g
- Saturated Fat: 0.5g
- Cholesterol: 0mg
- Sodium: 60mg
- Total Carbohydrates: 23g
- Dietary Fiber: 3g
- Sugars: 16g
- Protein: 1g

Note: Nutrition information is approximate and may vary based on specific ingredients used.

87. Therefore I Am Tahini Toast

Inspired by the bold and unique spirit of Billie Eilish, the "Therefore I Am Tahini Toast" is a delicious and nutritious twist on the classic toast. This recipe reflects Billie's creativity and individuality, offering a satisfying blend of flavors and textures. Packed with wholesome ingredients, this toast is not just a treat for your taste buds but also a celebration of self-expression.

Serving: 2 servings
Preparation Time: 5 minutes
Ready Time: 10 minutes

Ingredients:
- 4 slices of whole grain bread
- 1/2 cup tahini
- 1 ripe avocado, sliced
- 1 tablespoon lemon juice
- 1 teaspoon red pepper flakes
- Salt and pepper, to taste
- 2 radishes, thinly sliced
- Fresh cilantro leaves, for garnish
- Optional: sesame seeds for extra crunch

Instructions:
1. Toast the Bread:
- Toast the whole grain bread slices to your desired level of crispiness.
2. Prepare Tahini Spread:
- In a small bowl, mix the tahini with lemon juice, salt, and pepper. Adjust the seasoning to taste.
3. Spread Tahini:
- Spread a generous layer of the tahini mixture on each toasted slice of bread.
4. Add Avocado Slices:
- Place avocado slices evenly on top of the tahini spread.

5. Season and Garnish:
- Sprinkle red pepper flakes over the avocado for a hint of heat.
- Arrange radish slices on the toast for a refreshing crunch.
- Garnish with fresh cilantro leaves and sesame seeds if desired.
6. Serve:
- Serve the "Therefore I Am Tahini Toast" immediately, allowing the creamy tahini, ripe avocado, and crunchy radishes to create a symphony of flavors and textures.

Nutrition Information (per serving):
- Calories: 320 kcal
- Protein: 9g
- Fat: 20g
- Carbohydrates: 30g
- Fiber: 8g
- Sugar: 2g
- Sodium: 280mg

This delightful toast not only pays homage to Billie Eilish's unique style but also offers a nutritious and satisfying meal that can be enjoyed any time of the day.

88. Bad Guy Broccoli Bites

Embrace the bold and rebellious flavors of Billie Eilish with these "Bad Guy Broccoli Bites." Inspired by Billie's edgy and unapologetic style, these savory bites are the perfect fusion of attitude and wholesome goodness. Packed with the undeniable charm of broccoli and a hint of spice, these bites are a tribute to the bad guys who make life interesting.

Serving: Makes approximately 20 broccoli bites.
Preparation Time: 15 minutes
Ready Time: 30 minutes

Ingredients:
- 3 cups broccoli florets, finely chopped
- 1 cup breadcrumbs
- 1/2 cup grated Parmesan cheese
- 2 large eggs

- 2 cloves garlic, minced
- 1 teaspoon smoked paprika
- 1/2 teaspoon cayenne pepper (adjust to taste)
- Salt and pepper to taste
- Olive oil for baking

Instructions:
1. Preheat your oven to 375°F (190°C). Line a baking sheet with parchment paper and set aside.
2. In a large mixing bowl, combine the finely chopped broccoli, breadcrumbs, grated Parmesan cheese, minced garlic, smoked paprika, cayenne pepper, salt, and pepper.
3. In a separate bowl, beat the eggs and then add them to the broccoli mixture. Mix well until all ingredients are evenly combined.
4. Take a small portion of the mixture and shape it into bite-sized balls, placing them on the prepared baking sheet.
5. Lightly brush each broccoli bite with olive oil to enhance crispiness.
6. Bake in the preheated oven for 20-25 minutes or until the edges are golden brown and the bites are firm to the touch.
7. Allow the Bad Guy Broccoli Bites to cool for a few minutes before serving.

Nutrition Information:
(Per serving - 4 bites)
- Calories: 180
- Protein: 9g
- Carbohydrates: 20g
- Fiber: 4g
- Sugars: 2g
- Fat: 8g
- Saturated Fat: 2g
- Cholesterol: 45mg
- Sodium: 350mg

Feel free to adjust the seasonings according to your taste preferences, and enjoy these Bad Guy Broccoli Bites as a rebellious twist to your snack repertoire!

89. Happier Than Ever Honeydew Hors d'oeuvres

Get ready to embark on a delectable journey with our "Happier Than Ever Honeydew Hors d'oeuvres," inspired by the soulful and innovative Billie Eilish. These bite-sized wonders are a celebration of flavors that will leave you feeling as euphoric as Billie's chart-topping hits. With the refreshing essence of honeydew and a touch of creativity, this appetizer is a harmonious blend of sweet and savory that will make your taste buds sing.

Serving: Makes approximately 20 hors d'oeuvres.
Preparation Time: 15 minutes
Ready Time: 30 minutes

Ingredients:
- 1 small honeydew melon
- 200g feta cheese, crumbled
- 1/4 cup fresh mint leaves, finely chopped
- 1/4 cup balsamic glaze
- 1/4 cup honey
- 1 French baguette, thinly sliced
- Olive oil for brushing
- Salt and pepper to taste

Instructions:
1. Prepare the Honeydew: Cut the honeydew melon in half, remove the seeds, and use a melon baller to scoop out small, bite-sized melon balls. Place them in a large bowl.
2. Mix with Feta and Mint: Add the crumbled feta and finely chopped mint leaves to the bowl with the honeydew balls. Gently toss the ingredients together until well combined.
3. Prepare Baguette Slices: Preheat your oven to 350°F (175°C). Arrange the thinly sliced baguette on a baking sheet. Brush each slice lightly with olive oil and sprinkle with a pinch of salt. Toast in the oven for about 10 minutes or until the edges are golden brown.
4. Assemble the Hors d'oeuvres: Take each toasted baguette slice and top it with a spoonful of the honeydew, feta, and mint mixture.
5. Drizzle with Balsamic Glaze and Honey: Drizzle balsamic glaze and honey over each hors d'oeuvre for an extra burst of flavor. Be generous but delicate to maintain the balance of sweet and savory.

6. Serve: Arrange the Happier Than Ever Honeydew Hors d'oeuvres on a serving platter and delight in the symphony of flavors.

Nutrition Information:
(Per Serving)
- Calories: 120
- Total Fat: 5g
- Saturated Fat: 2.5g
- Cholesterol: 15mg
- Sodium: 180mg
- Total Carbohydrates: 18g
- Dietary Fiber: 1g
- Sugars: 10g
- Protein: 3g

Elevate your culinary experience with these Happier Than Ever Honeydew Hors d'oeuvres, a tribute to the creativity and uniqueness of Billie Eilish's musical artistry. Enjoy the delightful combination of honeydew, feta, and mint that promises to leave you happier than ever.

90. Your Power Yellowfin Tuna Tacos

Embrace the bold and vibrant flavors of Billie Eilish's world with "Your Power Yellowfin Tuna Tacos." These tacos are a celebration of individuality and self-expression, much like Billie's music. Packed with fresh ingredients and a zesty kick, these tacos are a culinary journey that echoes the eclectic beats of Billie's music.

Serving: Makes 4 servings
Preparation Time: 20 minutes
Ready Time: 30 minutes

Ingredients:
- 1 lb fresh yellowfin tuna, sushi-grade, diced
- 8 small corn tortillas
- 1 cup red cabbage, thinly shredded
- 1 ripe mango, diced
- 1 avocado, sliced
- 1/4 cup red onion, finely chopped

- 1/4 cup cilantro, chopped
- 1 jalapeño, thinly sliced (optional for heat)
- 2 limes, cut into wedges

For the Marinade:
- 2 tablespoons soy sauce
- 1 tablespoon sesame oil
- 1 tablespoon honey
- 1 teaspoon fresh ginger, grated
- 1 garlic clove, minced
- Salt and pepper to taste

Instructions:

1. Prepare the Marinade:
In a bowl, whisk together soy sauce, sesame oil, honey, grated ginger, minced garlic, salt, and pepper. This will be the flavorful marinade for the yellowfin tuna.

2. Marinate the Yellowfin Tuna:
Place the diced yellowfin tuna in a bowl and pour the marinade over it. Gently toss to ensure the tuna is well-coated. Allow it to marinate for at least 10 minutes in the refrigerator.

3. Heat the Tortillas:
Warm the corn tortillas in a dry skillet over medium heat for about 10-15 seconds on each side or until they are pliable. Alternatively, you can heat them in the oven or microwave.

4. Assemble the Tacos:
Take the marinated yellowfin tuna and distribute it evenly among the warm tortillas. Top with shredded red cabbage, diced mango, avocado slices, chopped red onion, cilantro, and jalapeño slices if you desire some heat.

5. Garnish and Serve:
Squeeze fresh lime juice over the tacos and garnish with additional cilantro. The vibrant colors and flavors are a tribute to Billie's artistic style.

Nutrition Information:

Per Serving (2 Tacos):
- Calories: 350
- Protein: 25g
- Carbohydrates: 30g
- Fiber: 6g

- Sugars: 10g
- Fat: 15g
- Saturated Fat: 2g
- Cholesterol: 40mg
- Sodium: 500mg

Note: Adjust the spice level by controlling the amount of jalapeño added. These tacos are a burst of freshness and flavor, perfect for those who appreciate the creativity and uniqueness that both Billie Eilish and a well-crafted dish bring to the table.

91. NDA Nectarine Napoleon

Indulge in the sweet symphony of flavors with the NDA Nectarine Napoleon, a dessert inspired by the bold and eclectic taste of Billie Eilish. Named after her hit single "NDA," this culinary creation is a delightful melody of juicy nectarines, flaky puff pastry, and luscious vanilla cream. Elevate your dessert game with this harmonious blend of textures and tastes that pays homage to Billie's unique style.

Serving: Serves 4
Preparation Time: 20 minutes
Ready Time: 40 minutes

Ingredients:
- 2 sheets of puff pastry, thawed
- 4 ripe nectarines, sliced
- 1 cup heavy cream
- 1/2 cup powdered sugar
- 1 teaspoon vanilla extract
- 1/4 cup sliced almonds, toasted
- Mint leaves for garnish (optional)

Instructions:
1. Preheat your oven to 400°F (200°C).
2. Roll out the puff pastry sheets on a floured surface. Using a sharp knife, cut each sheet into 4 equal squares. Place the pastry squares on a parchment-lined baking sheet.

3. Bake the puff pastry according to the package instructions until golden brown and puffed up. Allow it to cool completely.

4. While the pastry is baking, whip the heavy cream in a chilled bowl until soft peaks form. Add the powdered sugar and vanilla extract, continuing to whip until stiff peaks form.

5. Once the puff pastry has cooled, assemble the napoleons. Place a pastry square on a serving plate, add a dollop of whipped cream, and layer with sliced nectarines. Repeat the process with another pastry square and more layers until you have a beautiful stack.

6. Finish the napoleons by dusting the top with powdered sugar and sprinkling toasted sliced almonds. Garnish with mint leaves if desired.

7. Serve immediately and savor the symphony of flavors in each bite.

Nutrition Information:

(Per serving)

- Calories: 420
- Fat: 28g
- Saturated Fat: 11g
- Cholesterol: 61mg
- Sodium: 154mg
- Carbohydrates: 38g
- Fiber: 3g
- Sugar: 14g
- Protein: 5g

Note: Nutrition information is approximate and may vary based on specific ingredients used. Adjustments can be made to meet dietary preferences.

92. Not My Responsibility Noodle Nest

Indulge in the rebellious spirit of Billie Eilish with our "Not My Responsibility Noodle Nest" – a dish that's as bold and unapologetic as the artist herself. This noodle creation is a fusion of flavors that dance on the palate, mirroring Billie's eclectic musical style. So, channel your inner nonconformist and prepare to savor the rebellious notes of this culinary delight.

Serving: 4 servings

Preparation Time: 15 minutes
Ready Time: 30 minutes

Ingredients:
- 8 oz thin egg noodles
- 2 tbsp vegetable oil
- 1 cup shiitake mushrooms, sliced
- 1 cup red bell pepper, julienned
- 1 cup broccoli florets
- 1/2 cup shredded carrots
- 2 cloves garlic, minced
- 1/4 cup soy sauce
- 2 tbsp oyster sauce
- 1 tbsp hoisin sauce
- 1 tsp sesame oil
- 1/2 tsp red pepper flakes (adjust to taste)
- 1 green onion, thinly sliced (for garnish)
- Sesame seeds (for garnish)

Instructions:
1. Boil Noodles: Cook the thin egg noodles according to the package instructions. Drain and set aside.
2. Sauté Vegetables: In a large skillet or wok, heat vegetable oil over medium-high heat. Add sliced shiitake mushrooms, julienned red bell pepper, broccoli florets, shredded carrots, and minced garlic. Stir-fry for 5-7 minutes or until the vegetables are tender-crisp.
3. Prepare Sauce: In a small bowl, whisk together soy sauce, oyster sauce, hoisin sauce, sesame oil, and red pepper flakes.
4. Combine Noodles and Sauce: Add the cooked noodles to the skillet with the sautéed vegetables. Pour the sauce over the noodles and vegetables, tossing everything together until well coated and heated through.
5. Serve: Divide the Not My Responsibility Noodle Nest among plates. Garnish with thinly sliced green onions and sesame seeds for an extra burst of flavor and texture.
6. Enjoy: Embrace the rebellious spirit as you savor each bite of this unique noodle creation inspired by the one and only Billie Eilish.

Nutrition Information (per serving):
- Calories: 320

- Total Fat: 8g
- Saturated Fat: 1g
- Trans Fat: 0g
- Cholesterol: 55mg
- Sodium: 950mg
- Total Carbohydrates: 50g
- Dietary Fiber: 4g
- Sugars: 3g
- Protein: 12g

Note: Nutrition information is approximate and may vary based on specific ingredients used.

93. Overheated Orange Olive Oil Cake

Billie Eilish, with her eclectic style and unique personality, has inspired a generation with her music. In the spirit of her creativity, we present the "Overheated Orange Olive Oil Cake." This dessert is a symphony of flavors, combining the warmth of olive oil, the zest of oranges, and a touch of Billie's signature boldness. It's a treat that harmonizes with her dynamic artistry, making every bite a musical experience.

Serving: 8-10 servings
Preparation Time: 20 minutes
Ready Time: 1 hour 30 minutes

Ingredients:
- 2 cups all-purpose flour
- 1 1/2 cups granulated sugar
- 1 teaspoon baking powder
- 1/2 teaspoon baking soda
- 1/2 teaspoon salt
- 1 cup extra virgin olive oil
- 1 cup fresh orange juice
- Zest of 2 oranges
- 4 large eggs
- 1 teaspoon vanilla extract
- Powdered sugar for dusting (optional)

Instructions:
1. Preheat your oven to 350°F (175°C). Grease and flour a 9-inch round cake pan.
2. In a large bowl, whisk together the flour, sugar, baking powder, baking soda, and salt.
3. In a separate bowl, combine the olive oil, orange juice, orange zest, eggs, and vanilla extract. Mix well until the ingredients are thoroughly combined.
4. Gradually add the wet ingredients to the dry ingredients, stirring until just combined. Be careful not to overmix.
5. Pour the batter into the prepared cake pan, spreading it evenly.
6. Bake in the preheated oven for 50-60 minutes or until a toothpick inserted into the center comes out clean.
7. Allow the cake to cool in the pan for 15 minutes before transferring it to a wire rack to cool completely.
8. Once cooled, you can dust the top with powdered sugar for a decorative touch.

Nutrition Information (per serving):
- Calories: 380
- Total Fat: 22g
- Saturated Fat: 3g
- Trans Fat: 0g
- Cholesterol: 70mg
- Sodium: 230mg
- Total Carbohydrates: 42g
- Dietary Fiber: 1g
- Sugars: 25g
- Protein: 5g

This "Overheated Orange Olive Oil Cake" is a delightful blend of sweet and citrusy notes, capturing the essence of Billie Eilish's bold and vibrant energy. Enjoy this dessert as a tribute to the musical genius herself!

94. Copycat Coconut Curry

Embrace the vibrant and eclectic flavors that resonate with the spirit of Billie Eilish with our Copycat Coconut Curry recipe. Just like Billie's music, this dish is a fusion of bold and unexpected elements that come together harmoniously. The creamy coconut base provides a luxurious backdrop for an array of spices, creating a melody of tastes that will leave your taste buds singing.

Serving: 4 servings
Preparation Time: 15 minutes
Ready Time: 45 minutes

Ingredients:
- 2 tablespoons coconut oil
- 1 large onion, finely chopped
- 3 cloves garlic, minced
- 1 tablespoon fresh ginger, grated
- 2 tablespoons red curry paste
- 1 teaspoon turmeric powder
- 1 teaspoon cumin powder
- 1 teaspoon coriander powder
- 1 teaspoon paprika
- 1 can (14 oz) coconut milk
- 1 cup vegetable broth
- 1 pound boneless, skinless chicken thighs, cut into bite-sized pieces (substitute tofu for a vegetarian option)
- 1 cup broccoli florets
- 1 bell pepper, thinly sliced
- 1 carrot, thinly sliced
- Salt and pepper to taste
- Fresh cilantro, chopped, for garnish
- Cooked jasmine rice, for serving

Instructions:
1. In a large pan, heat the coconut oil over medium heat. Add the chopped onion and sauté until translucent.
2. Add the minced garlic and grated ginger to the pan. Sauté for an additional 2 minutes until fragrant.
3. Stir in the red curry paste, turmeric, cumin, coriander, and paprika. Cook for 2-3 minutes to allow the spices to bloom.
4. Pour in the coconut milk and vegetable broth, stirring to combine. Bring the mixture to a simmer.
5. Add the chicken pieces (or tofu) to the pan and cook until browned on all sides.

6. Toss in the broccoli, bell pepper, and carrot slices. Simmer until the vegetables are tender, about 15-20 minutes.

7. Season the curry with salt and pepper to taste. Adjust the spice level by adding more curry paste if desired.

8. Serve the coconut curry over cooked jasmine rice. Garnish with fresh cilantro.

Nutrition Information:
(Per serving)
- Calories: 480
- Protein: 25g
- Carbohydrates: 25g
- Fat: 32g
- Saturated Fat: 25g
- Cholesterol: 90mg
- Sodium: 650mg
- Fiber: 5g
- Sugar: 6g

Immerse yourself in the soulful blend of flavors inspired by the creativity of Billie Eilish with this Copycat Coconut Curry – a dish that's as unique and memorable as her music.

95. I Didn't Change My Number Iced Latte

Indulge your taste buds with the "I Didn't Change My Number Iced Latte," a refreshing coffee creation inspired by the bold and eclectic style of Billie Eilish. This energizing beverage combines the rich flavors of espresso with a touch of sweetness, making it the perfect companion for those moments when you want to savor a sip of something special.

Serving: 2 servings
Preparation Time: 5 minutes
Ready Time: 10 minutes

Ingredients:
- 2 shots of espresso (or 1/2 cup strong brewed coffee, chilled)
- 1 cup of cold milk (dairy or non-dairy)
- 2 tablespoons of sweetened condensed milk

- 1/2 teaspoon of vanilla extract
- Ice cubes
- Optional: whipped cream and chocolate shavings for garnish

Instructions:
1. Brew two shots of espresso or prepare 1/2 cup of strong brewed coffee and let it cool to room temperature.
2. In a mixing bowl, combine the cold milk, sweetened condensed milk, and vanilla extract. Stir until well blended.
3. Fill two glasses with ice cubes, ensuring there's enough space for the liquid.
4. Pour one shot of espresso (or 1/4 cup of strong brewed coffee) into each glass over the ice.
5. Slowly pour the milk mixture over the espresso, allowing it to cascade over the ice.
6. If desired, top the iced latte with a dollop of whipped cream and a sprinkle of chocolate shavings.
7. Give it a gentle stir before sipping and enjoying the harmonious blend of coffee and sweetness.

Nutrition Information:
Note: Nutrition values are approximate and may vary based on specific ingredients and brands used.
- Serving Size: 1 drink
- Calories: 150
- Total Fat: 5g
- Saturated Fat: 3g
- Trans Fat: 0g
- Cholesterol: 20mg
- Sodium: 60mg
- Total Carbohydrates: 20g
- Dietary Fiber: 0g
- Sugars: 18g
- Protein: 5g

Feel free to adjust the sweetness and milk proportions to suit your taste preferences. Cheers to sipping on the "I Didn't Change My Number Iced Latte" and enjoying the rhythmic flavors inspired by Billie Eilish!

Inspired by Billie Eilish's whimsical and unique style, these "Ilomilo Iceberg Lettuce Cups" are a playful and refreshing twist on traditional appetizers. Named after one of Billie's iconic songs, these lettuce cups are a perfect blend of crispiness, flavor, and creativity. Enjoy a bite-sized burst of freshness that echoes Billie's boundary-pushing approach to music.

Serving: Makes 4 servings.
Preparation Time: 15 minutes.
Ready Time: 15 minutes.

Ingredients:
- 1 head iceberg lettuce
- 1 cup cherry tomatoes, diced
- 1 cup cucumber, finely chopped
- 1/2 cup red onion, minced
- 1/2 cup bell peppers (any color), diced
- 1/2 cup feta cheese, crumbled
- 1/4 cup black olives, sliced
- 1/4 cup fresh parsley, chopped
- 1/4 cup extra virgin olive oil
- 2 tablespoons balsamic vinegar
- Salt and pepper to taste

Instructions:
1. Prepare the Lettuce Cups:
- Carefully remove the outer leaves of the iceberg lettuce to create cups. Trim the edges for a neat appearance.
2. Prepare the Filling:
- In a mixing bowl, combine cherry tomatoes, cucumber, red onion, bell peppers, feta cheese, black olives, and fresh parsley.
3. Make the Dressing:
- In a small bowl, whisk together extra virgin olive oil, balsamic vinegar, salt, and pepper.
4. Assemble the Cups:
- Spoon the vegetable and feta mixture into each lettuce cup, creating a colorful and vibrant presentation.
5. Drizzle with Dressing:

- Drizzle the balsamic dressing over the filled lettuce cups, ensuring an even distribution of flavors.
6. Serve:
- Arrange the Ilomilo Iceberg Lettuce Cups on a serving platter and serve immediately. The crispiness of the lettuce paired with the fresh and tangy flavors will be a delightful experience.

Nutrition Information:
Per Serving
- Calories: 180
- Total Fat: 14g
- Saturated Fat: 4g
- Trans Fat: 0g
- Cholesterol: 15mg
- Sodium: 280mg
- Total Carbohydrates: 10g
- Dietary Fiber: 3g
- Sugars: 5g
- Protein: 5g

These Ilomilo Iceberg Lettuce Cups are a tribute to Billie Eilish's innovative spirit. Perfect for a light and tasty appetizer, they embody the essence of Billie's eclectic style, inviting you to savor every refreshing bite.

97. Lost Cause Limeade

Indulge in the rebellious spirit of Billie Eilish with the refreshing and bold "Lost Cause Limeade." This vibrant concoction is inspired by the singer's fearless attitude and eclectic style. Perfect for those who love a burst of flavor and a touch of rebellion, this limeade is a delightful twist on a classic favorite.

Serving: Serves 4
Preparation Time: 15 minutes
Ready Time: 2 hours (including chilling time)

Ingredients:
- 1 cup fresh lime juice (approximately 8-10 limes)

- 1 cup granulated sugar
- 4 cups cold water
- 1 teaspoon lime zest
- 1/2 cup fresh mint leaves, loosely packed
- Ice cubes for serving
- Lime slices and mint sprigs for garnish

Instructions:
1. Prepare the Limeade Base:
- In a small saucepan, combine the granulated sugar with 1 cup of water. Heat over medium heat, stirring until the sugar completely dissolves. Remove from heat and let it cool to room temperature to create a simple syrup.
2. Mixing the Limeade:
- In a large pitcher, combine the fresh lime juice, simple syrup, and the remaining 3 cups of cold water. Stir well to combine.
3. Infuse with Mint:
- Add the lime zest and fresh mint leaves to the pitcher. Use a muddler or the back of a spoon to gently crush the mint leaves, releasing their flavor into the limeade.
4. Chill and Infuse:
- Cover the pitcher and refrigerate for at least 2 hours, allowing the flavors to meld and the limeade to chill thoroughly.
5. Serve:
- Fill glasses with ice cubes and pour the chilled Lost Cause Limeade over the ice.
6. Garnish:
- Garnish each glass with a slice of lime and a sprig of mint for a visually appealing touch.

Nutrition Information:
- *Serving Size:* 1 cup
- *Calories:* 120
- *Total Fat:* 0g
- *Cholesterol:* 0mg
- *Sodium:* 5mg
- *Total Carbohydrates:* 32g
- *Dietary Fiber:* 0g
- *Sugars:* 29g
- *Protein:* 0g

Elevate your taste buds with the Lost Cause Limeade – a beverage that mirrors the audacious spirit of Billie Eilish in every sip. Perfect for a sunny day or a lively gathering, this limeade is a tribute to those who appreciate a blend of boldness and zest in their culinary adventures.

98. Ocean Eyes Olive and Onion Omelette

Indulge in the rich, savory melody of flavors with our "Ocean Eyes Olive and Onion Omelette," inspired by the hauntingly beautiful songstress, Billie Eilish. This dish captures the essence of Billie's soulful music, combining the briny allure of olives with the sweet notes of caramelized onions. It's a symphony of tastes that will make your taste buds dance to the rhythm of the sea.

Serving: This recipe serves 2.
Preparation Time: 15 minutes
Ready Time: 25 minutes

Ingredients:
- 4 large eggs
- 1/4 cup diced black olives
- 1/4 cup diced green olives
- 1/2 cup finely chopped onions
- 1/4 cup shredded Parmesan cheese
- 2 tablespoons olive oil
- Salt and pepper to taste
- Fresh parsley for garnish (optional)

Instructions:
1. Prep the Ingredients:
- Crack the eggs into a bowl and beat them until well combined.
- Dice the black and green olives, finely chop the onions, and shred the Parmesan cheese.
2. Caramelize the Onions:
- Heat 1 tablespoon of olive oil in a non-stick skillet over medium heat.
- Add the chopped onions and sauté until they turn golden brown and caramelized, about 5-7 minutes.
- Remove the onions from the skillet and set them aside.

3. Cook the Omelette:
- In the same skillet, add the remaining 1 tablespoon of olive oil and heat it over medium-low heat.
- Pour the beaten eggs into the skillet, tilting it to ensure even distribution.
- Sprinkle the caramelized onions, diced olives, and shredded Parmesan evenly over the eggs.
- Season with salt and pepper to taste.
4. Fold and Finish:
- Allow the omelette to cook undisturbed until the edges set, about 3-4 minutes.
- Carefully fold the omelette in half using a spatula.
- Cook for an additional 2-3 minutes or until the eggs are fully cooked and the cheese is melted.
5. Serve:
- Slide the Ocean Eyes Olive and Onion Omelette onto a serving plate.
- Garnish with fresh parsley if desired.

Nutrition Information:
(Per Serving)
- Calories: 320 kcal
- Protein: 18g
- Fat: 25g
- Carbohydrates: 6g
- Fiber: 2g
- Sugar: 2g
- Sodium: 580mg

Elevate your breakfast experience with this unique omelette that harmonizes the diverse flavors inspired by the eclectic sounds of Billie Eilish. Enjoy the taste of the ocean with every delightful bite!

CONCLUSION

"Eilish Eats: A Culinary Symphony of 98 Inspired Recipes" isn't just a cookbook; it's a testament to the vibrant fusion of music, artistry, and gastronomy. The 98 food ideas curated in this culinary journey celebrate the essence of Billie Eilish, encapsulating her creativity, innovation, and boldness in every dish.

Each recipe within these pages embodies the diverse spectrum of Billie's music and persona, translating her eclectic style into tantalizing flavors, textures, and presentations. Just as Billie's music defies boundaries, these recipes transcend the conventional, inviting readers to explore a world where culinary imagination knows no limits.

From "Bad Guy Brownies" to "Ocean Eyes Oysters," the cookbook weaves a tapestry of flavors inspired by Billie's iconic songs, lyrics, and experiences. Each recipe is a harmonious blend of ingredients, much like the layers of emotions and sounds in her music. Whether it's the savory "When the Party's Over Pasta" or the sweet and sour "Bellyache BBQ Ribs," every dish captures a unique aspect of Billie's artistry.

What sets "Eilish Eats" apart is its ability to resonate with both seasoned chefs and enthusiastic beginners. The recipes are crafted to be accessible yet imaginative, encouraging experimentation and creativity in the kitchen. The cookbook not only serves as a guide to cooking but also as an avenue for self-expression, mirroring the authenticity and fearlessness that Billie Eilish embodies.

Moreover, this collection transcends mere recipes; it's a culinary voyage that fosters a sense of community and connection. Through these dishes, fans and food enthusiasts alike can bond over a shared love for Billie's music while indulging in delightful gastronomic adventures. The cookbook bridges the gap between music and food, illustrating how art in one form can inspire artistry in another.

Beyond the delightful flavors and innovative recipes, "Eilish Eats" stands as a tribute to creativity and individuality. It encourages readers to embrace their uniqueness, just as Billie fearlessly embraces hers. The cookbook serves as a reminder that innovation knows no bounds and that inspiration can stem from the most unexpected places, including the melodies and rhythms that resonate in our hearts.

As the final page of "Eilish Eats" turns, it leaves a lingering taste of inspiration, urging readers to not just follow recipes but to create their own symphonies in the kitchen. It's an invitation to infuse every dish with personal flair and imagination, much like Billie infuses her music with raw emotion and authenticity.

In essence, "Eilish Eats: A Culinary Symphony of 98 Inspired Recipes" is not just a cookbook—it's a celebration of art, individuality, and the boundless possibilities that arise when music and food intertwine. It's a testament to the transformative power of creativity and the magic that happens when passion meets the palate. It's an ode to Billie Eilish, her music, and the flavors that echo her spirit—a culinary journey that resonates long after the last recipe is savored.

Printed in Great Britain
by Amazon

41996030R00096